New Directions in Transactional Analysis Counselling

SITE COLLECTION

New Directions in Transactional Analysis Counselling

An Explorer's Handbook

DAVID MIDGLEY

FREE ASSOCIATION BOOKS/LONDON/NEW YORK

Published in 1999 by
Free Association Books Ltd
57 Warren Street, London W1P 5PA
and 70 Washington Square South,
New York NY 10012–1091

British Library Cataloguing in Publication Data
A CIP catalogue record for this book is available from the British
Library

ISBNs: 1 85343 430 2 hardback, 1 85343 429 9 pbk

Produced for Free Association Books by
Chase Production Services, Chadlington, OX7 3LN
Printed in the EC by T.J. International Ltd, Padstow

To Betty
for many years of good-humoured toleration
and an abundance of tender, loving care
in a marvellous marriage
that never really needed transactionally analysing.

Contents

Preface

Becoming a transactional analyst calls, ideally, for contributions from many teachers and practitioners so that the trainee gets a wide experience of different styles of working. Those to whom I am indebted are too many for me to mention them all individually but there are a few I must acknowledge by name, even at the risk of its reading like an exercise in name-dropping! First, Michael Reddy who led the 101 Introductory Course I attended in Birmingham in 1977, and who later taught me how to begin using TA principles in practical work with clients. Next came Gordon Law, my first sponsor and contracted teacher and supervisor, followed by Ian Stewart, Director now of the Berne Institute, whose first graduate trainee I am proud to be.

But there were many others, some of whom came to this country on teaching missions from the USA and elsewhere. They included Bob and Mary Goulding, Jaqui Schiff, Shea Schiff and Graham Barnes. A most valued home-based teacher who introduced me to Gestalt Therapy, as well as providing many hours of personal therapy, training, and supervision, was Petruska Clarkson. And Jenny Robinson, Director now of a residential TA facility in Birmingham for the treatment of young people with severe mental disturbances, gave me a great deal of help and encouragement as I followed her on the demanding road to 'clinical membership', as it used to be called. There were many, many others, but these in particular deserve a special mention.

But none of these illustrious people must be held in any way responsible for what I have written, though I have acknowledged them in the text as sources and included them wherever appropriate in the list of references.

I acknowledge also my debt to several good friends and colleagues who have been my supervisors during the course of more than thirty years as caseworker, counsellor, and psychotherapist; and to some thousands of clients, without whom nothing could have happened at all.

Acknowledgements

Permission to use copyright material is gratefully acknowledged to the following publishers and authors: Penguin UK for quotations from *Games People Play* (1968) and *A Layman's Guide to Psychiatry and Psychoanalysis* (1971) both by Eric Berne; Bantam Doubleday Dell, New York, for quotations from *What Do You Say After You Say Hello?* (1975) by Eric Berne; Souvenir Press, Ltd, London, for quotations from *Transactional Analysis in Psychotherapy* (1975) by Eric Berne; Bloomsbury Publishing, Plc, London, for a quotation from *Emotional Intelligence* by Daniel Goleman, 1996; Routledge, London, for quotations from *Transactional Analysis Psychotherapy – An Integrated Approach* (1992) by Petruska Clarkson; Routledge, London (ARK Paperback, 1990) for a quotation from *Modern Man in Search of a Soul* by C.G. Jung; Harpers College Press, New York, 1977 for a quotation from *Corrective Parenting in Private Practice* by Jon and Laurie Weiss in *TA After Eric Berne*, edited by Graham Barnes; Huron Valley Institute Press, Michigan, 1978, for quotations from *Transactional Analysis* by Stan Woollams and Michael Brown; Grove Press Inc., New York, 1998, and Mary McClure Golding, for quotations from *Changing Lives Through Redecision Therapy* by Robert and Mary Goulding; Harper & Row, New York, 1975, for quotations from *Cathexis Reader, TA Treatment of Psychosis* by Jaqui Schiff, et al.; Harper & Row, New York, 1977, for a quotation from *Egograms* by John Dusay; Nelson, London, 1968, for a quotation from *A Critical Dictionary of Psychoanalysis* by Charles Rycroft; Random House UK, Ltd (The Hogarth Press, 1949) for quotations from *An Outline of Psychoanalysis* by Sigmund Freud; Random House UK, Ltd, (Arrow Books, Ltd, 1990) for quotations from *The Road Less Travelled* by M. Scott Peck; Piatkus (Pub.) Ltd, London, 1991, for a quotation from *OK Parenting* by Mavis Klein; Spectrum Psychological Services, Ypsilanti, Michigan, 1977, for a quotation from *Psychodiagnosis in Brief* by Michael Brown; Real People Press, Moab, Utah, 1969, for quotations from *Gestalt Therapy Verbatim* by Frederick S. Perls; Harper Colophon, New York, 1970, for a quotation from *The Paradoxical Theory of Change* by Arnold Beisser in

Gestalt Therapy Now, ed. Joen Fagan and Irma Lee Shepherd; Grove Press, New York, 1974, for quotations from *Scripts People Live* by Claude Steiner; World Health Organization, 1978, for quotations from *ICD 9*, (Glossary and Guide to Classification of Diseases, 9th Revision); Addison Wesley, Reading, Mass., 1976, for a quotation from *Techniques in Transactional Analysis* by Muriel James; Boyce Productions, Trans. Pub., San Francisco, 1977, for quotations from *How to Cure – How Eric Berne Practiced Transactional Analysis* by Southey Swede; Oxford University Press, 1991, for a quotation from *The Ages of Gaia* by James Lovelock; The Transactional Analysis Journal, January, 1992, for a quotation from *In Praise of Speed, Experimentation, Agreeableness, Endurance and Excellence: Counterscript Drivers and Aspiration*, by Petruska Clarkson; *ITA News* for quotation from the following article by Petruska Clarkson: *Physis in Transactional Analysis*, No. 33, Summer, 1992

An account of Chapters 11 and 12 appeared as a two-part article in the Summer and Autumn, 1993, issues of *ITA News*, under the title 'Character Disorder – A TA Perspective'. These chapters and the original articles owe much to unpublished workshop presentations by Shea Schiff, for which the author is particularly grateful.

An account of Chapter 13 appeared as a two-part article in the Summer and Autumn, 1997, issues of *ITA News* under the title 'The Total Human Being – A Spiritual Perspective'.

Every effort has been made to obtain permission to use copyright material. However, several expressions, 'sayings' and diagrams have come into such general use in transactional analysis that it is not always possible to say where they originated. If proper acknowledgement has not been made in respect of any material included in this book, the publisher would appreciate advice of this so that the deficiency can be made good in future editions.

List of Diagrams

Introduction

Many people, especially those in the helping professions and voluntary counselling agencies, have already discovered transactional analysis. They are fascinated by the elegant simplicity with which human nature and relationships can be understood and graphically presented in simple diagrams. TA, as we usually call it for short, can even be presented so that children can understand it, and it is, therefore, used increasingly in the field of education. The organizational use of transactional analysis as a model for training in management and industry has been well established for many years. Certification in clinical or other special fields, however, can take years of training at a cost of several thousand pounds, and might not be a viable option for many.

There are a few substantial British texts readily available in the bookshops, and several American texts can be obtained without difficulty. These are essential reading for trainee transactional analysts in particular and others who need a comprehensive knowledge and understanding of TA theory. The present book, however, is designed for practitioners whose primary interest is in making practical use of TA in day-to-day casework and counselling and, perhaps, for psychotherapists who normally use a different model from transactional analysis. It is for those whose appetite might have been whetted by an exciting first encounter with TA and who would like to explore further and in more depth, with guidance on where to find more detailed accounts of certain aspects of TA if they need to.

This book, however, is addressed primarily to counsellors rather than to psychotherapists. Unfortunately, the terms 'counselling' and 'psychotherapy' are used interchangeably by some, and those who distinguish between them do not always define them in the same way. For example, counselling is widely used to mean 'advice giving' but the Code of Ethics of the British Association for Counselling states that 'counsellors do not normally give advice'! A dictionary definition of psychotherapy is 'the use of psychological methods to treat mental disorders' – but there is dispute among practitioners about what constitutes a mental disorder. And some restrict their use of the term 'psychotherapy' to psychoanalysis. A student counsellor, who consulted me about an essay she was writing on the difference between counselling and psychotherapy, suggested that it depended 'who was in the driving seat'. There's more to it than that, of course, but certainly the psychotherapist is likely to take more control of the direction of work once a contract has been agreed.

Since there is no universally accepted definition of either process I will state here that I use the term 'counselling' to mean the practice of helping people who are basically well adjusted to mobilize their personal resources in the interests of solving problems in many areas. These will include relationship problems, lack of self-esteem, bereavement, career problems, spiritual problems, relatively mild anxiety states and panic reactions, reactive depression, relatively mild character and personality disorders, and the distressing confusion that might occur on the heels of some personal trauma when the person needs, above all, to find a 'new direction' in life. By 'psychotherapy' I mean helping people whose essential mental adjustment has been damaged in some way (either developmentally or by traumatic experiences later in life) to make desirable changes in the way they think, feel, and behave. This includes the treatment of such conditions as chronic depression and severe anxiety states and phobias, for example, and more serious and deeply entrenched character and personality disorders – provided that the client is reasonably well motivated. Psychotherapy might also be used, by suitably trained practitioners, as part of the therapeutic process in treating some subjects with psychotic disturbances such as schizophrenia and manic depressive disease, where there is also a biochemical factor in the causation. Counselling and psychotherapy, however, are not mutually exclusive. Practitioners of one discipline will inevitably use elements of the other; so some of the material in this book, particularly in Part Two on Applied Transactional Analysis, might seem more appropriate for psychotherapy than for counselling.

This book is an experienced practitioner's account of how TA can be readily understood and how it can be used by counsellors in straightforward practical work with clients. It offers certain specific 'new directions' in transactional analysis which, to the best of my knowledge, have not been explored before in quite this way. The first of these is the New Ego State Model, which breaks with mainstream practice by using just one diagram to illustrate the structure and the function of ego states. Unfortunately, TA literature is strewn with inconsistencies in describing ego states, and this has led to confusion at the very foundations of transactional analysis. Chapter 2, therefore, is designed to clarify our understanding of what ego states are and what they do. While some practitioners who are committed to earlier conventions might find this disconcerting, I believe that the majority of readers, especially those relatively new to TA, will find the New Ego State Model helpful. A presentation and critique of several other ego state diagrams which appear in the mainstream literature, however, will be found in Appendix A for the interest of transactional analysts and other advanced practitioners.

A particular feature of the New Ego State Model is a re-appraisal of the Parent ego state, providing a possible 'new direction' for some practitioners who have, in the past, held it responsible for many human ills; and there is an invitation to see the essential qualities of parental nurture as embracing both care and control, including discipline and responsible criticism!

Arising from this re-appraisal of the Parent ego state is the recognition of character disorder – 'the flip side of neurosis' – as a condition that is far more commonly seen in counselling rooms at the turn of the millennium than it was in the 1960s, when transactional analysis first came on the scene. Chapters 11 and 12, in Part Two, incorporate material from a two-part article published in *ITA News* in 1993 under the title 'Character Disorder – a TA Perspective'.[1] These two chapters deal with the distinction between neurosis and character disorder, describe the TA understanding of character disorder in terms of deficiencies in the Parent ego state, and outline an approach to the management or possible treatment of the condition. Also in Part Two is an extended chapter on Practical Counselling that provides numerous ideas and techniques I have found useful. This chapter is not intended to make the book into a Do-it-Yourself treatment manual for those who are untrained and inexperienced in using counselling skills, although it does include guidance on some issues, such as ethics and supervision, which should be helpful to practitioners who are just starting out. The book is intended particularly to be of practical help to counsellors, caseworkers, therapists, and others in the helping professions who are already experienced in using some other approach. There is guidance in the text and in the references on where readers can find a more detailed account of many of the techniques referred to.

Part Three deals with the spiritual dimension of life, a 'new direction' that is already being discussed increasingly in counselling circles where the concept of 'spiritual' is widely associated with the notion of a 'core self'. Using a transactional analysis perspective, however, – and especially when taking into account Berne's concept of *Physis*, the growth force of nature 'which takes the happiness of others into consideration' – the 'new direction' suggested in this account gives greater emphasis to the human being in relationship – ideally in community – rather than to any notion of the total human being as self-sufficient, independent, and autonomous.

As I have already observed, there is no universally accepted distinction between counselling and psychotherapy, and the term 'psychotherapist' translates as 'doctor of souls'. Ours is an increasingly secular age in which traditional religion is failing to meet human need in all but a very small section of the community. Those suffering physical dis-ease will usually go to a doctor, but even many religious people suffering dis-ease in the area of mind, spirit, or relationships are more likely to visit a counsellor or therapist than a priest or minister. The counsellor, caseworker, or therapist is driven by the changing world we live in to perform a task that is, in my view, indisputably spiritual. How to respond to the hunger so many of my clients reveal, for a sense of selfhood which transcends the merely individual and seems to reach out to the *'other'*, and how to make secular sense of a whole dimension of life which is traditionally the province of institutional religion and to integrate this perception into my counselling work, is a challenge that the final part of this book begins to address. And it is one which I believe will become more and more urgent as we grow professionally and strive to help our clients become 'total human beings'.

Throughout the text, male or female personal pronouns are used interchangeably to avoid clumsy sentence construction but I trust that I might be forgiven, as a male of the species, if I favour the masculine gender in some passages!

It is my hope that this book will be an encouragement to practitioners seeking new therapeutic directions to help their clients and that they might even, perhaps, find in it some new directions for themselves.

David Midgley,
Certified Transactional Analyst,
UKCP Registered Psychotherapist,
BAC Accredited Counsellor.
Middlesbrough, July, 1998.

Part One:
Understanding Human Nature

1 A Brief Review of Ego States

More than thirty years ago, Eric Berne's book *Games People Play*[2] caught the public imagination and became a world best-seller. It was, of course, intended for mental health professionals as a follow-up to his *Transactional Analysis in Psychotherapy*[3] but, by the early 1960s, thousands of people were talking about 'Parent, Adult and Child' and TA was quickly regarded as something anybody could 'do'. This very superficial perception of transactional analysis was largely attributable to the use by popular writers of an over-simplified model of ego states. The Child ego state was presented as the feeling organ, the Adult as the thinking organ, and the Parent as the believing or behavioural organ. The reality, of course, is that thinking, feeling, and behaviour are interrelated dimensions of human experience in *any* ego state. The apparent easy accessibility of transactional analysis did nothing for its standing among academic psychotherapists! Only a few thoughtful people recognized that Berne had made one of those seminal observations that are destined to change the way human beings perceive themselves.

Human life is a continual battle between what we feel we *want* to do, which is the concern of the Child ego state, and what we believe we *ought* to do, which is the concern of the Parent ego state. The conflict may be resolved by the intervention of the Adult ego state, which is concerned with what is actually going on in reality. The Adult ego state then concerns itself with *how* to do whatever has been decided.

The simple three-ring diagram in Figure 1 represents these three ego states, or ways of being, which are common to all mature, well-adjusted people. It is the basic working tool of transactional analysts. The Child ego state is a way of thinking, feeling, and behaviour established during the first few years of life when a normal infant is curious, creative, adventurous, and highly intuitive. It is concerned first and foremost with survival and to that end has a natural disposition to experience and express joy, anger, fear, and sadness with freedom and spontaneity. As we shall see, however, we quickly learn that such uninhibited emotion is more than many parents can cope with!

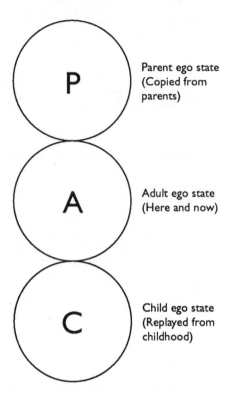

Parent ego state
(Copied from
parents)

Adult ego state
(Here and now)

Child ego state
(Replayed from
childhood)

Figure 1　Basic Ego State Model

The mature and integrated Adult ego state thinks, feels, and behaves in ways that are appropriate to what is actually going on here and now. It reasons, learns skills, feels compassion when faced with the suffering of others – and does something about it!

The Parent ego state is borrowed or copied from parents and other grown-ups and from a variety of social influences such as education and the media. It is the repository of beliefs and values about issues of right and wrong and of a learned pattern of how to nurture one's self and others.

Diagnostic clues to which ego state is being cathected – that is energized or activated – include the person's choice of words, tone of voice, facial expressions, gestures, or posture. The response of other people is also indicative. For example, someone using his Parent ego state is likely to provoke a Child ego state response in another person and vice versa. Also it is sometimes possible to observe a person behaving in a manner similar to one of his parents when he is in his Parent ego state; or to see a man of, say, thirty behaving in his Child ego state as he did when he was only five. Professional footballers do this whenever their side scores a goal!

Sometimes a person can become trapped in just one ego state and have no freedom to move appropriately to another ego state, as a well-adjusted person can. For example, some entertainers, especially comedians, function almost exclusively from a Child ego state and might seem to have little Adult from which to perceive the real world as it actually is. Some criminals also function largely from Child and Adult and might seem to have no Parent ego state at all to provide authentic care and control for either themselves or others. Some policemen, teachers, social workers, or prison officers might have a tendency to get trapped in their Parent ego state; and some accountants, lawyers, and engineers in their Adult. All these conditions can seriously affect relationships and might be an important area for contractual change in therapy.

Another problem occurs when a person's Adult presentation of self, or his perception of reality, is influenced, out of awareness, by feelings, thoughts, or behaviours from either the person's Parent or Child ego state. This is called contamination and in therapy it is essential to decontaminate by continual confrontation. This means drawing the attention of the Adult ego state to what is going on so that the person becomes aware of it and can do something about it.

For the practical, therapeutic use of transactional analysis, however, it is necessary to have an understanding of ego states that goes beyond this basic three-ring diagram. A primary purpose of the present book is to provide the relative newcomer to TA with a deeper understanding of ego states, and this will be dealt with in the next chapter. We can then build on this more comprehensive foundation, using the New Ego State Model in Figure 2 which will be found overleaf. You may find it useful to place a bookmark in the page to refer to the diagram again later.

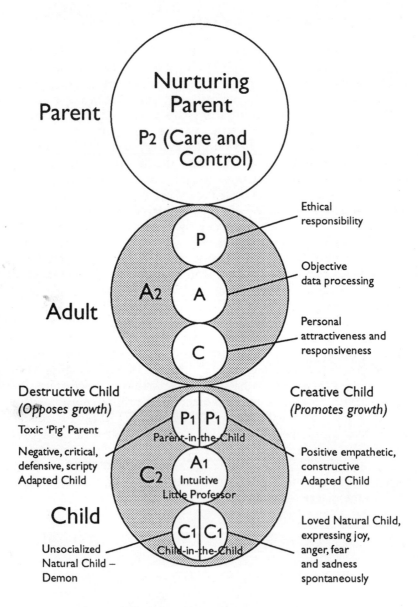

The Parent Ego State (P2) – Copied from Parents
The Adult Ego State (A2) – Here and Now Reality
The Child Ego State (C2) – Replayed from Childhood

Figure 2 A New Ego State Model

2 Ego States in Action

This chapter presents an analysis of ego states, what they consist of and what they do, using the New Ego State Model illustrated in the diagram in Figure 2. The simple basic ego state diagram in Figure 1 in Chapter 1, Eric Berne used to describe both the structure or content of ego states and also their function. But when it came to a more detailed analysis, he used one diagram for structure and a different one for function and this has been a continual source of confusion. The New Ego State Model used in this book is found in Figure 2 on p. 10. It is designed, like the basic model in Figure 1, to describe structure and function, and the chapter shows how the one arises *from* the other, because every structure has a function. So only one diagram is necessary. For the interest of advanced practitioners and trainees in transactional analysis the author's rationale for this decision is presented in Appendix A.

Ego is the Greek word for 'I' – so an ego state is simply a way of being 'me'. There are, in fact, thousands of possible ego states, not just three, even though they can all be classified under the three main divisions of Parent, Adult, and Child; and we think, feel, and behave in various ways in each of them. In this chapter we shall consider what an ego state *is* and also what it *does*. If we use the human body as an analogy, the study of what it is made of and how it is designed is the province of anatomy; the study of how it works is called physiology. But the human mind is at least as complex, subtle, and mysterious as the body it moves around in; probably it will become more so as our understanding of it grows.

Each basic ego state has a structure which is relatively fixed like that of the organs of the body; but, while the general pattern of an ego state is much the same from one personality to another, its more detailed structure, and consequently the way it functions, might vary enormously in different individuals. So while your heart or liver might be anatomically much the same as mine, and will serve exactly the same physiological or functional purposes, your Parent ego state might be different from mine in structure and in function. Even so, each would still be distinctively a Parent way of being and not a Child or Adult way.

How we behave or function in any ego state is at least partly due to what 'building blocks' have gone into its structure. For example, if, as children, we copied from a parent a controlling and bossy way of relating to people, then that parental contribution to our personality structure is likely to influence the way we function in relating to others in later life. People might comment that we are 'a chip off the old block'. But bossiness need not be our invariable style of functioning in our Parent ego state. On other occasions we might be very warm and supportive of others. This could equally be 'a chip off the old block' but possibly a different 'block' or parent figure, or even the same one on a different occasion. Whether we actually function as controlling and bossy or as warm and supportive in any particular situation will depend on other factors. A teacher in front of an unruly class might need to function as bossy and controlling to bring them into order; but the same teacher, five minutes later, might function as warm, supportive, and encouraging to a child who is genuinely struggling with a problem.

Similarly, techniques and strategies for problem-solving, which have been learnt from experience, will be remembered and built into the structure of the Adult ego state. These may then be brought into use functionally in appropriate circumstances. Which strategy is mobilized for functional use will depend on environmental factors, particularly the personalities of others with whom we are transacting.

The structure of the Child ego state includes consciously or unconsciously remembered experiences built on to a substratum of biological material which will be detailed below. How the Child ego state manifests functionally – that is, which of these building blocks will be 'triggered' in a later situation – is influenced by what is going on in that person's life at the time. This might be either an external reality (such as an overzealous traffic warden!) or an internal fantasy such as a fear of failure; or any of an infinite variety of other stimuli. So there is a continuing interaction between structure and function, each contributing to the other in various ways. It is, in my experience, unhelpful to regard structure and function as two distinct areas of reality.

With this general understanding of what an ego state is and what it does, we now consider how the human personality develops.

The New Ego State Model

Almost every account of ego states in the mainstream literature describes them from the top downwards, starting with the Parent. The account in this book, however, starts at the bottom and works upwards. So we begin by describing the Child ego state, or more specifically the Child-in-the-Child, where human growth and development does begin.

The New Ego State Model is based on one used by Claude Steiner, one of Berne's early associates, in his book *Scripts People Live*.[4] The diagram in this book is designed differently from Steiner's, however.

For certain therapeutic purposes, advanced practitioners of transactional analysis do need to understand the structure of the Parent ego state in more detail than this diagram provides, so a commonly used diagram showing this more detailed structure is included in Appendix A, Figure 11(d).

The Creative Child-in-the-Child Ego State

At birth we begin our lives, in normal circumstances, as nature intended us to be. To begin with this is a largely biological reality. We have an innate need of food, warmth, and Strokes (or recognition), and if these needs are adequately met, we will usually grow up with plenty of freedom to be our true selves. As infants our experience of the world is mainly in terms of bodily sensations and so the Child-in-the-Child is sometimes referred to as the Somatic Child, *soma* being the Greek word for body. This is a structural concept and is labelled C1 because it is the first Child ego state to manifest. Later on, other features will manifest and they will be labelled *collectively* as C2.

When we are born we obviously have only a Child ego state or Child way of thinking, feeling, and behaviour. If we are well nurtured by our parents, we will probably grow up with a fair degree of freedom to express functionally joy, anger, fear, and sadness when appropriate. These emotions are essential parts of our biological inheritance and each has an important role in ensuring our survival in certain circumstances. Our freedom to experience and express natural emotions appropriately will go a long way to ensuring our emotional and physical health and the integrity of our relationships when we are grown up. When we are actually expressing joy, anger, fear, or sadness appropriately we say we are, functionally, in our Natural or Free Child ego state. On the New Ego State Model this propensity is featured on the right-hand side at the bottom of the diagram. It is the 'Creative Loved Natural Child, expressing joy, anger, fear and sadness spontaneously' and its role is consistent with promoting the growth of the infant into adulthood.

Grown-up Experience of the Natural Child Ego State

Every experience, from the moment of birth and possibly even before, provides, at least potentially, a way of being or an ego state. So the manifestation of our Child ego state at the age of, say, forty, might be a replay of thoughts, feelings, and behaviours first experienced at the age of four. Equally, at the age of fifty-five we might replay thoughts, feelings, and behaviours first experienced at the age of two or six, for example. Which ego state is triggered – the four-year-old or the six-year-old – will be determined by the nature of the present circumstances. In certain kinds of therapeutic work it might be important for the client to re-live the original experience in fantasy or role-play. It is, therefore, important, for the therapist to recognize that there is more to Child ego states than merely being child-like 'in a general sort of way'.

The Destructive Child-in-the-Child Ego State

On the left of the diagram at the bottom is the 'Unsocialized Natural Child'. This ego state develops when the infant fails to receive good parenting with both Care and Control, and is probably what Berne called the Demon. In his last book, he wrote 'The Demon first appears in the high chair, when Jeder scatters his food on the floor with a merry glint, waiting to see what his parents will do. If they make friends with it, it will go on to later mischief and then perhaps into humorous fun and jokes. If they beat it down, it will lurk, surly, in the background, ready to leap out at an unguarded moment and scramble his life as it originally scrambled his food.'[5]

This unsocialized Natural Child is a predominant feature in the personality structure of delinquents and others whose aim in life is to 'have fun', regardless of the distress they cause to other people.

The Adult-in-the-Child

Like the Adult ego state described briefly in Chapter 1, the Adult-in-the-Child is concerned with what is going on in the real world 'out there'. But obviously he has very limited powers of understanding and interpreting whatever it is he becomes aware of. Nevertheless, this psychic organ is exceedingly wise and intuitive. He 'picks up the vibes', senses the emotional atmosphere, and 'knows' what people want or need of him or for themselves. In all probability he can pick up subliminal signals that grown-ups, being preoccupied with reason and logic, would miss. He is rather like a dog, which can hear and smell things in the real world that his more intelligent, reasoning master is quite oblivious to. In fact, the Adult-in-the-Child could be said to have, at least potentially, information-gathering antennae like a sputnik! It is because of his innate cleverness and astonishing intuition and wisdom that the Adult-in-the-Child is called the Little Professor.

People in certain professions, especially where imagination and creativity are called for, often have a particularly sensitive Little Professor. Detectives, for example, in reality as well as in Agatha Christie stories, often have 'hunches' that lead them into the best areas of investigation. So do counsellors and psychotherapists, for the matter of that; and perhaps orchestral conductors and the directors of stage or television dramas and other programmes who might 'just have a feeling' that one way of doing something would be better than another.

The Little Professor's intuitive feelings, perceptions, and experiences are recorded in the structure of the Adult-in-the-Child ego state, to be mobilized functionally when called upon in the future. However, the Little Professor does not usually appear as a separate ego state in diagrams of the functional model or in most egograms (*see* Appendix A). The reason for this is that the Little Professor does not function independently. He functions only in association with either the Child-in-the-Child or the Parent-in-the-Child, which we shall deal with next.

The Creative Parent-in-the-Child Ego State

When she is very little, a baby does not distinguish between herself and her mother. Her mother is 'in' her from the moment of birth or even, perhaps, from conception. As she develops an awareness of her separateness, the Parent-element remains and provides the basis of a way of being, or ego state, called the Parent-in-the-Child, labelled P1 on the New Ego State Model.

From the beginning of life, therefore, the youngster will have an option to experience and express functionally the Parent part of her or his Child ego state, labelled P1, as well as the Natural Child part, which is labelled C1. The early Parent structure is a primitive ego state that will soon begin to manifest parent-type characteristics. A little girl will nurse dollies, a little boy will trundle a toy wheelbarrow. Even as he takes his first steps, a visiting aunt might say, 'Look at that! He walks just like his daddy'.

But he does not just copy his daddy or a girl her mummy. In fact, each will copy and assimilate characteristics from both parents and also from others who might sometimes be in a parent-type relationship with them – older siblings and grandparents, for example. This also happens in the development of the Parent ego state (P2), as will be seen in the structural diagrams in Appendix A.

For purposes of communal living a youngster must learn to function in socially acceptable ways. So he will learn, for example, personal hygiene, to wash and to clean his teeth, and to eat without making a mess – unlike Berne's Jeder! He will learn to speak and to use socially acceptable language, to be reasonably courteous in his dealings with grown-ups, and to treat other children also with respect. As he learns to do these things he is responding to a Parent voice in his own head so that he will eventually wash his hands before a meal and clean his teeth afterwards even if his mother does not actually tell him to do so. He is 'programmed'. But not quite like a computer because he is free – in principle, at least – to decide to ignore the programming on some occasions and to act differently.

A particularly valuable adaptation invested in the Creative Parent-in-the-Child is the quality of empathy. This is the capacity to sense or feel what someone else is feeling. As indicated above, the Adult-in-the-Child will contribute to this. In addition, empathy is probably modelled to some extent by the youngster's parents. If they are sensitive to his or her needs and feelings, then the youngster will develop the desire and the capacity to be sensitive to the needs and feelings of others. Obviously, this is a great asset in terms of personal relationships, and is especially important for those of us in people-oriented jobs, such as therapists and caseworkers, teachers, ministers, counsellors, and many others. 'Failure to register another's feelings', says Daniel Goleman, 'is a major deficit in emotional intelligence, and a tragic failing in what it means to be human. For all rapport, the root of caring, stems from emotional attunement, from the capacity for empathy.'[6] When these Parent-in-the-Child characteristics manifest functionally they are referred to as the Adapted Child ego state. So care should be taken not to regard everything associated with the Adapted Child as negative.

The Destructive Parent-in-the-Child

This ego state – again manifesting functionally as the Adapted Child – is at the heart of a great deal of human unhappiness, broken relationships, and mental pathology. When the youngster – or the grown-up person cathecting (that is, using) a Child ego state – is under threat, the urgent question arises, 'How am I going to handle this?' The threat might be of being assaulted in some way, of someone leaving home, or of being forced, perhaps, into some scary situation. The Little Professor then goes into action, collecting and collating information – hard facts, vibes, recorded memories of similar experiences from the past – and decides on a course of action. This might be a 'natural' solution involving the free and uninhibited use of anger, fear, sadness, or joy; or it might be an 'adapted' solution, involving the use of some substitute feeling – a Racket Feeling, which will be discussed in a later chapter.

Children develop a range of operational Child ego state (C2) strategies for dealing with emergencies by taking account of what they believe (rightly or wrongly) their parents and other parent figures require or expect of them. As we have just seen, this can provide for the very valuable capacity for empathy. But frequently children learn to respond to the needs and demands of others in a way that is seriously detrimental to their own personal growth. The messages a little child picks up through the sensitivity of her Little Professor, may come from different ego states in her or his parents. If they come from a parent's Parent ego state (P2, detailed below) they will normally introduce the youngster to socially acceptable ideas of right and wrong which promote growth. For example, a little girl will be rewarded with smiles and praise for not soiling her nappies or for using the potty. Or she might be scolded with mother's angry voice and censure if she throws down her feeding dish and makes a mess. Children must adapt to these authentic and authoritative voices from mother and from father (the parents' Parent ego states) and learn to obey them if they are to survive and continue to enjoy parental affection and social approval.

But, if the messages come from the parents' Child ego states (as illustrated in the Script Matrix diagrams in Figure 7, p. 47), they are probably designed to control the youngster *for the parents' sake*, rather than for the sake of their son's or daughter's well-being. These messages can be very toxic indeed and might be seriously detrimental to the interests, welfare, and personal growth of the youngster. They are likely to be incorporated into the Negative Parent-in-the-Child ego state of the youngster where they become the subject of an Early Decision, as we shall see in the chapter on Script formation, and will oppose normal growth and personal development.

All these early messages from parents and others are programmed into the structure of the Child ego state, and form elements of the Parent-in-the-Child or P1 on the New Ego State Model. Whatever has been programmed in structurally can, however, also manifest functionally in relationships with other people or even introspectively in fantasy in the person's private thoughts and feelings. When the stored messages and Early Decisions go 'into action' (with the Little

Professor's wise guidance) to meet the emergency, the result is called Adapted Child behaviour. This means, essentially, the Child ego state adapted to solve problems in a manner that meets the supposed needs or demands of parents and other authority figures. For example, a youngster might discover from experience that, when he whines helplessly that he can't perform some task such as, for example, tying his shoe laces, someone will do it for him. On an odd occasion this probably signifies nothing but, if he goes on whining and finding that people respond by doing things for him, the behaviour will be reinforced. Later, in grown-up life, when faced with the troublesome task of arranging his annual domestic budget, he might revert to whining helplessly until his wife offers to do it for him! Helplessness is a mode of Negative Adapted Child behaviour. Other typical modes of adaptation include help*ful*ness (doing things unnecessarily for people well able to help themselves) and hurtfulness. All three of these behaviours suggest Game-Playing roles.

Other typical Child adaptations are compliance, withdrawal, rebellion, and procrastination. The ways a person in his Child ego state might adapt in the face of difficulties are legion, however. The determining factor is the creative ingenuity of the Little Professor, or Adult-in-the-Child, which acts in co-operation with the Parent-in-the-Child to work out clever ways of surviving, often by manipulating other people.

If the Child response is spontaneous and intended to meet his or her *own* needs rather than someone else's, however, then it is called Free Child or Natural Child (i.e., un-adapted) behaviour.

The Adult Ego State

As already indicated in Chapter 1, the Adult ego state deals with the realities of what is actually going on here and now. Some early TA writers have defined the Adult as a computer that takes in information about the real world, processes it, stores it, and uses it to estimate probabilities, to reason things out, and to solve problems. It does, indeed, do these things but, like the Parent and Child ego states, it can also have feelings that are appropriate to the reality of what is actually going on, and it can respond sensitively to the needs of others.

The Adult ego state can manifest characteristics of personal attractiveness and responsiveness that are similar to those of a Natural Child ego state. Furthermore, the Adult ego state can have a sense of ethical responsibility which is comparable to that of a strong Parent ego state [*see* 'Ethos' in Figure 11(e)]. This means that a person can observe from his Adult ego state that, for example, there is distress in his community because of poverty, discrimination, or ecological factors, and he can make entirely Adult decisions, perhaps through the medium of politics, to do something about it. The notion of an 'Integrated Adult', which incorporates Parent and Child features as well as data-processing functions, has led some people to suppose that a really mature person could dispense with the Parent (P2) and Child (C2) ego states altogether. It is doubtful whether this could ever happen in practice but, if it did, then the resulting personality would, I think, lack the essential warmth that is characteristic of the 'total human being' as described in Part Three of this book.

Techniques and strategies for problem solving, which have been learnt from experience, will be remembered and built into the structure of the Adult ego state together with a range of skills associated with a variety of different activities. These can then be brought into use functionally in appropriate situations. Which strategy is mobilized for functional use will depend on circumstances and environmental factors. For example, a medical student will absorb a great deal of factual information into her Adult ego state during the course of her training to become a doctor. But, when she is faced with a patient who has broken a leg, the knowledge she will utilize will be different from the knowledge useful in treating someone with tonsillitis. Similarly, a social worker who has absorbed knowledge in the field of psychology, law, social policy, etc., will have a range of skills available, some of which will be appropriate for helping a client who is elderly or physically disabled and others appropriate to counselling a mother whose child has been caught using Ecstacy. Such practical differentials apply in all walks of life, including household management, personal relationships, or changing a wheel on the car. Some will call for an Adult awareness of ethical responsibilities, others for storing and computing information and yet others – the skills of personal relationships, for example – for personal attractiveness and responsiveness. On the New Ego State Model these behaviours are associated with a Parent, an Adult, and a Child function arising within the structure of the Adult ego state (A2).

Care and Control

The first few paragraphs of this chapter provided a general outline of how ego states, including the Parent ego state, develop and function. Each one of us might have in the structure of P2 hundreds of 'Parent' ego states and many ways of functioning parentally, either towards children or towards grown-up people – or even towards ourselves.

But the essential features of *any* Parent ego state are Care and Control. We noted that, while the teacher with an unruly class might draw on structural contributions from her father (who might have been an army sergeant) to bring the class under control, she could switch five minutes later to a warm and caring mode of parenting (derived, perhaps, from her affectionate mother) to help a child struggling with a problem. Both these Parent functions are essential to effective nurturing. The teacher cannot care for the children if she does not have control and she cannot control them creatively if she does not care for them.

So the term Nurturing Parent is used in this account (following the example of Claude Steiner)[4] not to distinguish this parental function from the controlling function, with which it is generally compatible, but to distinguish it from the negative and toxic Critical Parent, which arises from P1 and is associated with (but is not the same as) the Adapted Child ego state. *Collins English Dictionary* defines nurture as 'the act or process of promoting the development, etc., of a child'; and as 'to educate or train'.[7] Each of these functions requires elements of care and of control and it is, I believe, a misuse of language to place them in opposition to each other. Eric Berne and others have distinguished between Nurturing and Controlling Parent ego state functions. Unfortunately, this distinction was introduced to the public in the 1960s, at a time when any kind of parental control was felt by many to be an intolerable imposition and contrary to the general mood of liberation that was reacting against it. During the same period, society was becoming more and more sensitive to political issues of social discrimination. Because the Parent ego state was rightly seen as the repository of beliefs and values – some, but by no means all, of which were logically unsustainable – the Controlling aspect of the Parent ego state came to be associated with prejudice and so was generally referred to disparagingly. This is not to say that prejudice, when it occurs, is clinically unimportant; far from it! But it must be seen in proper perspective if the controlling aspect of the Parent ego state is to be accorded its real value. Nurturing came to be associated in particular with giving a youngster permission to grow and develop as an individual, a function that could then be extended into adult relationships – but only, it seemed, in the absence of either control or criticism! Freedom was, in fact, all too often confused with indulgence!

The term Critical Parent was widely used in those early days, rather than Controlling Parent, which was Berne's term. Nevertheless, the idea that the Nurturing Parent was positive and the Controlling Parent negative was widely taught and enthusiastically received, especially by many who had had a bad experience of parenting and who – possibly because of it – sought help from trans-actional analysis. More recent experience has, of course, shown that control and responsible, constructive criticism are equally necessary features of good parenting, and society has discovered to its cost the consequences of their being withheld.

The functions of Care and Control are so essential to the nurture of growing children that they are written into Child Care law. 'Care', says the *Children and Young Persons Act*, 1969[8] 'includes protection and guidance; and control includes discipline.' Although the wording has been changed in recent legislation, the 'care and control' require-ment is retained. If a child is found by the courts to be in need of either care or control, then he or she might be made subject to a Supervision Order or even taken into the care of the Local Authority.

Neurosis and character disorder are general diagnostic categories arising from the over- or underdevelopment of P2. This important consideration is dealt with in Chapters 11 and 12.

The Nurturing Parent

The Nurturing Parent, therefore, comprises both caring and control-ling aspects. Unlike the distinction between the Free or Natural Child and the Adapted Child ego states, care and control are not alternative functions for dealing with the same situation; both might be appropriate at the same time.

What is actually incorporated into the structure of the Parent ego state does, of course, vary from generation to generation and from one culture to another but there is a considerable degree of consis-tency. Many elements in The Ten Commandments, for example, are to be found in the codes of conduct of virtually all human societies throughout history, regardless of race, religion, and culture. Without strict rules prohibiting stealing, murder, and adultery, and requiring respect for parents, the continuance of communal living, whether in complex industrial societies or primitive animist communities, would be virtually impossible. Whether or not God carved them on tablets of stone might be arguable but there is no doubt that they – and many other moral precepts – are the distillation of thousands of years of human wisdom and experience.

These are big issues. But there are many smaller issues which are nevertheless important for successful living and the smooth running of society and which may be programmed into P2. A woman seeing a small hole appear in a garment is likely to recall her mother teaching her that 'a stitch in time saves nine' and will repair it before it gets too big. Thousands of 'messages' of this kind are programmed into the Parent ego state along with precepts such as 'work hard', 'honesty is the best policy', and 'health is better than wealth', to mention but three. Many such guidelines for living are passed down from parents to children in the form of proverbs, unless the familial links are broken – as frequently happens in modern Western society.

But the Parent ego state is not as *fixed* as the Child. It is subject to continual updating so that, for example, the Victorian teaching that 'a child should be seen and not heard' has now been largely discarded. 'Many hands make light work' might be recalled in an emergency but, at the end of many parties, the dirty dishes are now simply piled into the dishwasher! Parental prohibitions against extra-marital sex were virtually universal up to the 1960s, even though they were disregarded by many. Sexual freedom is still not the 'norm' in the sociological sense[7] but Parent programming in this regard, except, perhaps, in some religious communities, has become much more permissive.

Which Parent Ego State?

An important skill for the therapist – and, indeed, for the client – is that of distinguishing between the Parent ego state (P2) and the Parent-in-the-Child ego state (P1) and the functions arising from them. These two ego states can be described functionally as the Nurturing Parent (derived from P2) and the Adapted Child (derived from P1 – with A1 'guidance'). The Parent-in-the-Child is not, strictly speaking, the same as the Adapted Child – though Claude Steiner declares that it is![4] P1 is a vast assembly of memories of child-hood experiences, including Early Decisions, which can have a profound influence, without our being aware of it, on the way we think, feel, and behave. How we actually think, feel, and behave in our Child ego state, however, might be either an uninhibited Natural Child response to the situation we are in or, alternatively, an Adapted Child response based on childhood experiences that might have been more or less threatening to the youngster. The choice of which ego state to use and which mode of adaptation is a matter for the Little Professor (A1).

The essential difference between P2 and P1 functions is that P2 is concerned with the spiritual well-being of one's self, other persons, or of society at large while P1, even in its positive and creative aspects, is primarily concerned with the interests of the biological self.

It is sometimes hard to distinguish between the Nurturing Parent and the positive and creative functions of the Adapted Child, which are derived from P1. Among these is the capacity for empathy already referred to. But the Negative Adapted Child – or Pig Parent, as Steiner calls it – is usually easy to distinguish from the well-meaning control aspect of the Nurturing Parent, which is manifestly functioning in the interests of someone else, be it an individual or society in general. This does not mean, of course, that the Nurturing Parent always gets it right, but that the *intention* is benign, even when the beliefs and values manifest as prejudice and result in discrimination. It is important in transactional analysis to distinguish (politically as well as psychologically) between prejudice arising from P1, that is rooted in self-interest, and sincere (even if erroneous) beliefs that are held and promoted with the welfare of others in mind, including the welfare of society at large. Claude Steiner expresses it well, saying 'The fundamental difference between them [P1 and P2] is their potency, their value in human relationships, or, for lack of a "scientific" word, their goodness.'[4] Unfortunately, parents' concepts of 'goodness' cannot always be reconciled with those of their children, especially children of a generation often taught to believe that 'right' and 'wrong' are false categories and that we must all work out our moral values for ourselves.

The distinctive feature of ego states is that they can be seen and heard and observed in action. Understanding them is the very foundation of transactional analysis, and it is particularly important to have a proper understanding of the structure and of the function of the Parent ego states. With these foundations firmly laid, however, we can now go on to consider how our awareness and use of ego states can change and enhance the pattern of our relationships and the quality of our lives.

3 Analysing Transactions

Most of the personal, domestic, social, and political problems in the world are due, in the final analysis, to our failure to communicate effectively with one another. This usually means that one of us, at least, is using an inappropriate or a contaminated ego state. Each of us has three different basic ego states from which to address other people and they have three different ego states from which to respond. Also, we can now consider which *part* of an ego state a person is using – for example, is it the Child-in-the-Child (C1) or the Parent-in-the-Child (P1)? So there are several options available for use in communication.

There are three basic kinds of transactions:

1 Parallel transactions;

2 Crossed transactions;

3 Ulterior transactions.

If a person asks for information, he is usually speaking from his Adult ego state and is addressing the Adult of the other person. The question, 'What's the best route to Birmingham?' will probably result in sensible advice based on experience. This would be an Adult to Adult parallel transaction, the response coming from the ego state that was addressed (Figure 3a).

But, if the response comes back from an ego state different from the one addressed, we will have a crossed transaction (Figure 4b). Crossed transactions are the source of an enormous amount of conflict! For example:

KEVIN: What time is it? (A–A)
TERRY: Time you learned to say please. (P–C)

An ulterior transaction operates on two levels – the social level, which is apparently open and above board, and the psychological level which has a secret agenda. For example:

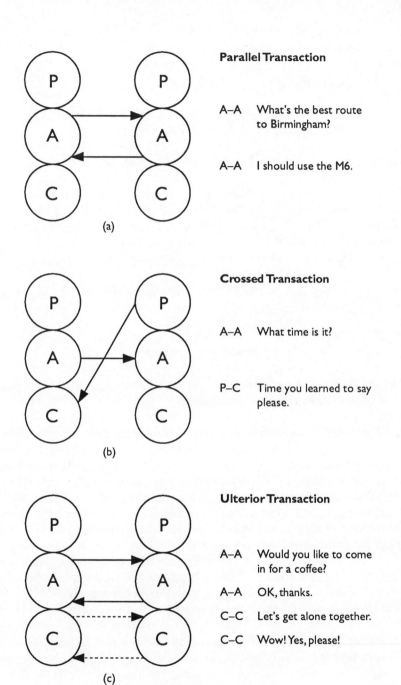

Parallel Transaction

A–A   What's the best route
       to Birmingham?

A–A   I should use the M6.

Crossed Transaction

A–A   What time is it?

P–C   Time you learned to say
       please.

Ulterior Transaction

A–A   Would you like to come
       in for a coffee?

A–A   OK, thanks.

C–C   Let's get alone together.

C–C   Wow! Yes, please!

Figure 3 Transactional Diagrams

Social Stimulus: (A–A) Would you like to come in for a coffee?
Social Response: (A–A) OK, thanks.

The secret meaning, however, might be:

Psychological Stimulus: (C–C) Let's get alone together.
Psychological Response: (C–C) Wow! Yes please!

American comedian Woody Allen is reputed to have said that 'coffee' is an obscene word!

Ulterior transactions like this are often the opening move in a psychological Game, to be discussed in Chapter 5. They are diagrammed as in Figure 3(c), the dotted line indicating the ulterior 'message' – frequently Child to Child but not necessarily.

There are three rules of communication in TA. They are:

1 If a transaction is complementary (parallel) communication can go on indefinitely.

2 If a transaction is crossed, communication will break down, at least temporarily, or something different will happen.

3 The outcome of a transaction will be determined at the psychological, rather than the social, level.

We usually refer to the analysis of transactions as 'Transactional Analysis Proper' to distinguish it from the whole system of TA. It is quite obvious that recognizing what kind of transactions are taking place in ordinary day-to-day interactions can have very far-reaching implications indeed. A proper understanding of what is actually happening when two people talk together can open up exciting possibilities for change in the way we get on with each other, the way we negotiate and solve problems – or fail to solve them.

There are many situations in therapy and counselling when the use of one or the other of these kinds of transactions is especially useful. For example, if a client is functioning from a whiny Adapted Child ego state, inviting the therapist to respond from Parent, it might be constructive for the therapist to cross the transaction by responding from Adult. I have sometimes used this technique when telephoned by a distressed client who weeps helplessly on the phone. To get her into Adult I might ask her to describe in detail the room she is phoning from, to give me a factual account of the day's events or perhaps to work out some mental calculation. By crossing the transaction in this way it is often possible to 'jog' the client into an Adult ego state so that 'something different' will happen and she can then, perhaps, begin practical problem solving instead of helpless whining.

4 A Stroke in Time

Stroking

A Stroke, in TA, is anything you do or say to someone by which you give them recognition. There are three basic kinds of Strokes – Physical, Verbal, and Non-verbal. Physical Strokes involve actual touching; Verbal Strokes depend on the things we say to each other and how we say them; Non-verbal Strokes may be given and received by looks, gestures, facial expressions, and many much more socially complex ways of treating one another. Simply to listen attentively when someone is talking to us is a powerful means of Stroking them non-verbally. An employee who is given a pay increase is Stroked by his employer, perhaps non-verbally, with just a note in his pay packet. So, paradoxically, is one who gets paid off, though the Stroke in that case is negative. The unstroked employee is one who is passed over, ignored, or taken for granted. He might eventually begin to wonder whether he really exists! A husband who makes a nice meal for his wife or a woman who buys a present for her partner are both giving positive Strokes.

Strokes can be positive or negative, conditional or unconditional. An appreciative glance is a Positive Non-verbal Conditional Stroke, conditional upon what we've done to 'deserve' such appreciation. 'You look a mess in that old suit' is a Negative Verbal Conditional Stroke – conditional upon the state of the suit. 'I love you' is an Unconditional Positive Verbal Stroke.

Positive Strokes, promoting good feelings, are obviously the best and these are the kind collected by Winners. People who collect no Strokes at all might get no feelings at all and that is almost the same as being dead. So people who fail to get many Positive Strokes are likely to behave in such a way as to collect Negative Strokes as an alternative means of psychological survival. Observers often say, 'Ignore him. He's only seeking attention!' He is, of course; but in those circumstances it is not always the best response to make sure he doesn't get any! It is better to teach him how to get Positive Strokes.

Strokes are as necessary to human life as other primary biological needs such as food, water, and shelter. And yet many people actually bring up their children to believe it is wrong to exchange Positive Strokes and good feelings because to do so might render them vulnerable to exploitation and a prey to all kinds of dangers. So they will tell their children not to smile at strangers, not to accept sweets from them, and certainly not to get into their cars! In a society like ours this is common sense, of course; but it tends to create people who are reluctant to speak at all unless they know each other very well. Consequently, many ordinary, law-abiding citizens who are desperately in need of love and friendship simply cannot get it!

Many people learn from early childhood how to survive on Negative Strokes and bad feelings. The experts at collecting Negative Strokes are usually accomplished Game-players, and they might become Losers whose lives are marked by one tragedy or 'misfortune' after another.

Claude Steiner, in *Scripts People Live*,[4] describes 'The Stroke Economy' by which we might bring up our children to an experience of lovelessness with five basic rules – *Don't give strokes, Don't ask for strokes, Don't accept strokes if you want them, Don't reject strokes if you don't want them*, and *Don't give yourself strokes*.

Time Structuring

There is a saying in TA that 'if a child is not stroked his spinal cord will shrivel up' – he will die, at least psychologically. Because getting enough Strokes to make life worthwhile is a survival issue, we tend to structure our time with Stroke-collecting in mind.

There are six ways we structure our time: Withdrawal, Rituals, Pastimes, Activity (or Work), Games, and Intimacy. Withdrawal is a way of structuring time that does not involve transactions with other people. The person disengages from whatever is going on and withdraws into himself. Watching television, reading a book, going to sleep or 'switching off' for a few moments in a lecture are all examples of Withdrawal. Not many Strokes are collected when we Withdraw from engagement with the world but we can Stroke ourselves to some extent and get either good or bad feelings doing it.

Rituals are transactions which are predictable, like saying Hello when we meet someone or shaking hands. Sharing a family meal round the table or going to the pub at 9 o'clock each evening can be mere Rituals but they provide more Strokes than Withdrawing into a hypnotic engagement with the television screen. A traditional church service can be a Ritual, sometimes quite a complex one; or the opening of proceedings in a court of law or in Parliament. In fact, just being where other people are and interacting with them in virtual silence, perhaps saying no more than 'Hi!' or 'Will you pass the salt?' is more rewarding in terms of Stroke uptake than cutting ourselves off from the world.

If, at the pub, a man talks with someone about cars or football they are Pastiming together, and that gets them more Strokes (good feelings) than drinking alone in silence. Pastimes are simply ways of passing time with other people, talking about things but not actually doing anything in particular.

A few examples of the Pastimes which Berne mentions in *Games People Play*[2] will be helpful because these ways of passing time are useful for sounding people out to discover who might be a likely Game-playing partner and good for Strokes, even if negative ones! Each Pastime, like each Game, has a name that indicates quite clearly what is going on. PTA means, of course, Parent-Teacher Association. In this Pastime parents talk about their children – or perhaps wives about husbands they regard as children! General Motors is a Pastime popular among men when they meet in pubs or at parties and talk about cars. At the same time groups of women might get together to play Grocery, Kitchen, or Wardrobe. But these exchanges are cautious, low-key engagements in which the participants avoid any serious emotional involvement. In fact, avoiding emotional involvement is what a Pastime is all about. Most casual conversations never get beyond that but, from time to time in the course of a Pastime, one comes across someone who is good for Strokes, and then we can go in any of three directions: Activities, Games, or Intimacy.

The essential feature of Activity (or Work), is that the people involved have a purpose and an agreed goal. It is an even more fruitful source of Strokes than Pastiming and often offers the rewards of achievement. Two men going into the pub car park to tinker with a carburettor are into Activity (or Work). They might become close friends, and the potential for Stroke-uptake is greatly enhanced.

Game-playing, described in the next section, is a very fruitful source of *negative* Strokes and *bad* feelings. Losers often spend a lot of time at it, especially if they fail to get many Strokes out of other ways of structuring their time.

Intimacy in TA means the sharing of thoughts and feelings with someone else in complete honesty and trust, using all our ego states as appropriate. It is an encounter between one total human being and another. It is the richest source of Positive Strokes and good feelings. But it is, of course, risky, and many parents advise their children against it by precept and by example. Eric Berne declared in one of his memorable aphorisms, that 'no-one spends more than fifteen minutes in Intimacy in an entire lifetime'! We must hope that this is not true for all, but it is probably true for many if not most.

An important consideration in therapy, therefore, is in exploring how the client structures her time and how fruitful is her present pattern of Time-structuring in getting her plenty of Positive Strokes. This is particularly important in the treatment of depression but it should never be neglected, whatever the presenting problem.

5 Analysing Games

There are scores of psychological Games with which people cause varying degrees of unhappiness to themselves and others. In his famous book *Games People Play*,[2] Eric Berne lists thirty or so and describes how we might play these Games to set up our own bad Racket Feelings. As with Pastimes, their names, such as Uproar, Kick Me, and Rapo, indicate what is going on.

The Game Formula

Berne used the Game Formula to describe the sequence of events in a psychological Game:

$$G + C = R - S - X - P$$

C stands for 'Con' – that is the psychological trick by which one person hooks another person into playing a Game. This involves a Discount, or non-verbal ulterior message to which he expects the other person to respond. For example, he might say 'Let me help you', appointing himself as Rescuer and Discounting the reality that the person really does not need to be helped.

G stands for 'Gimmick'. This is the person's weak spot or point of vulnerability, where he's wide open to being conned into a Game. For example, he might think of himself as being helpless and so welcomes 'help'.

R stands for 'Response'. This is a series of social messages, in parallel transactions, in which A helps B. It might go on for quite a long time.

S stands for Switch. Each player switches ego states or Game roles. Helpful 'A' suddenly realizes he's being exploited, turns nasty, and starts Persecuting 'B'. 'A', who started as a Victim seeking a Rescuer is now a Victim with a Persecutor!

X stands for Crossup – a moment of confusion in which both players wonder what ever happened. They had not consciously intended such an outcome!

P stands for Pay-off. This is the 'prize' at the end of the Game in which each player experiences a familiar bad feeling – the Racket Feeling which we shall deal with in the next chapter.

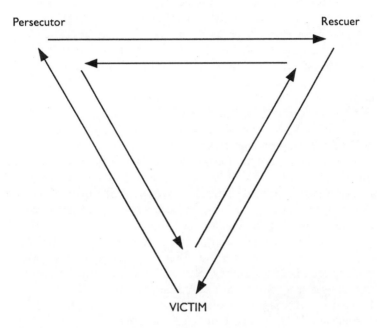

Figure 4 The Drama Triangle

The Drama Triangle

One of Berne's co-workers, Stephen Karpman, used the Drama Triangle to explain the process of Games. As in the diagram in Figure 4, there are three roles in a Game: Persecutor, Rescuer, and Victim, more in certain Games, such as those alcoholics play.[9]

A Game often played in therapy groups is called 'Why don't you ... Yes, but ...'. In this Game the person who is 'It' comes on as Victim and presents a problem to which the group members, accepting the role of Rescuer, suggest solutions. But 'It' rejects every suggestion until the group gets sick of it and begins to feel victimized. 'It' has switched from being Victim to being Persecutor and the group has switched from being Rescuer to being Victim! Everybody feels bad about it and experiences a Racket Feeling.

In the Game of Kick Me, someone begins by Discounting himself – that is, not taking into account his ability to solve a problem. His whole demeanour says 'Don't kick me, I'm very sensitive' and he appoints himself as the Victim. By his manner he invites or 'hooks' the other player into the Rescuer role. Victim might say, 'Every time I touch the electrics I get the wires crossed'. To which Rescuer (who prides himself on being good at electrics, so is vulnerable to this invitation) says, 'Never mind. Just leave that to me', and takes over. This might go on for some time until one day Rescuer begins to feel that he is doing all the work. He will then switch to Persecutor with an angry outburst such as 'There's the manual. Work it out for yourself!' The Kick Me player will then feel kicked. His Basic Life Position (see Chapter 7) of 'I'm not OK – You're OK' will be reinforced and his Script (see Chapter 8) will be advanced.

NIGYSOB is an acronym meaning Now, I've Got You, You Son Of a Bitch! It may be that Rescuer in the last example (Kick Me) is playing this Game. The Persecutor in NIGYSOB has frequently spent his whole life looking for opportunities to vent his rage on any available Victim. Some Victims, however, will unconsciously seek out an employer who is a born Persecutor; or he might even marry one, thus ensuring a regular supply of negative Strokes. The Persecutor's Racket Feeling pay-off might be a feeling of triumph but it is not a happy, 'OK' feeling. Victim's pay-off is a boost to his prevailing feeling of inferiority. NIGYSOB is a popular marital Game where the players' Scripts are scheduled to end in divorce.

Uproar is a Game played often by fathers and their teenage daughters in certain households. Consider the moves:

1 Daughter feels Victimized in her inferior teenage status and nominates her father as Persecutor.

2 She then switches to Persecutor herself by staying out late and her father then feels like a Victim in his anxiety.

3 Daughter arrives home at 2 a.m. and father immediately switches to Persecutor with 'What time do you call this!'

4 A violent row follows which ends with one or both parties going into the bedroom and slamming the door.

5 Both feel bad about it and experience their preferred Racket Feeling – daughter resentful, father angry – and both advance their Scripts.

Uproar can be played by any two people who fear that too much intimacy in their relationship could be dangerous. Brothers and sisters frequently play it.

Discounting

A Game begins when someone Discounts themselves, someone else, or reality. The reason why we do this is because the Child in us needs to maintain a frame of reference, or way of perceiving the world, which fits the Script we established when we were very little. One way of doing this is to leave some element of reality out of account – that is to Discount.

I find the best way to understand this is by reference to *The Healthy Model* described by Jon and Laurie Weiss.[10] They say:

> The emotionally healthy person is one who
> takes initiative to solve problems
> in a manner which *takes into account*
> his own needs, feelings, thoughts or behaviour,
> the needs, feelings, thoughts or behaviour of
> other persons and the reality of
> what is actually going on.

To 'not take account' of these things is to Discount and that is how Games often begin. It is helpful if married couples, partners, or parents and children learn how to Confront each other 'from an OK position' – that is, telling each other in an Adult way when they *feel* Discounted. I sometimes offer them a codeword (HALIFAX is the one I usually suggest) by which they can say 'I feel discounted' without blaming the feeling (which is really their own choice) on the other person. This idea should not be used without proper preparation, however, otherwise the parties can actually use it as a Persecution Game in itself![11]

First-degree Games are commonly played in ordinary day-to-day interactions; they hurt to some extent but don't usually damage. Second-degree Games can be much more painful and might result in a serious breakdown in relationships. Third-degree Games can literally be lethal, involving at least tissue damage and sometimes even death.

6 Rackets and Racket Feelings

Sigmund Freud used classical Greek mythology to provide many of the technical terms of psychoanalysis. This could be justified on the grounds that much of the mythology reflected, in symbolic language, human experience which he believed to be universal and the common lot of humankind. Unfortunately, however, it was understandable only to those who were 'educated'. Eric Berne had little patience with the esoteric language his medical colleagues used to communicate with one another while keeping their patients in the dark! Instead he preferred the language of fairy tales and nursery rhymes, and sometimes the terminology of the criminal underworld with which most people were familiar through Hollywood and the media. Berne expected his patients to be actively involved in their own treatment and invented terminology that would help them to know what was going on.

Hence the term 'Racket'. This term seems to have two origins. One was the ticker-tape machine which chattered away in the corner of the typical American office before the days of fax, e-mail, and the internet. So long as the machine was working and its 'racket' could be heard in the background, the office staff could get on with their work. But, if it broke down and the racket stopped, everyone would be vaguely uncomfortable and unable to settle to their work until an engineer had been called in to repair the ticker-tape machine and set it chattering again with its familiar background 'racket'. The other meaning of the term 'Racket' is still in use. It is the criminal underworld racket by which people are manipulated into paying money to the criminals in return for 'protection' from unwelcome criminal attention.

Strictly speaking, a Racket in transactional analysis is a set of manipulative behaviours unconsciously intended to set up a familiar bad feeling, in the hope that another person will be caused to change in some way. The bad feeling pay-off, which comes at the end of a Game, is called a Racket Feeling. The authentic and appropriate feelings we really want to express – perhaps joy, anger, fear, or sadness – were, as mentioned earlier, often suppressed in childhood.

Parents would demand 'good manners' or 'self-control' or a 'stiff upper lip', or demand to know, 'What are you looking so happy about?' As children, we would then adapt by deciding to have another feeling instead – perhaps guilt or helplessness – which seemed to be either acceptable to our parents or a better option for survival.

The four basic feelings of joy, anger, sadness, and fear each have a natural purpose when expressed appropriately.[12] Authentic joy needs no justification or motive. It is rooted in the human spirit and can be experienced and expressed by some people even when the outward circumstances are anything but congenial. Anger, however, is intended to change something which is happening *now*, perhaps someone else's bad behaviour. For example, a teacher faced with a class of unruly children might be angry in order to bring them into line, after which she can stop being angry and get on with the lesson. Fear is intended to provoke us into avoiding something that threatens to happen in the *future*. For example, a man who fears redundancy is likely to look for a new job before redundancy happens; if he fears a charging bull he will run away! Sadness is the feeling that accompanies grieving; it is nature's way of helping us deal with some loss that has occured in the *past*. This might be the death of someone we love, the failure of a relationship such as a marriage, or even the loss of some part of our body through accident or disease.

If these feelings are experienced and expressed spontaneously and appropriately, we can get them over with and then go on to something else, though sadness often takes much longer to fulfil its purpose than would fear or anger. But if, as sometimes happens, we feel anger in response to a loss instead of sadness, or fear when someone else's bad behaviour actually justifies anger, then we cannot 'get it over with' because the feeling is inappropriate and has served no useful purpose. It is a Racket Feeling and is likely to go on and on, smouldering away as a background feeling of muted misery.

There are many other feelings, usually rackety, that tend to be associated with certain Life Positions and that serve no useful purpose when it comes to problem solving. Figure 5 indicates some of the Racket Feelings that are typically associated with the Life Positions, to be dealt with in the next chapter.

There is no hard and fast rule about which Racket Feelings tend to be associated with which Life Position. We often have 'mixed feelings' in relation to certain situations and might sometimes switch fairly rapidly from one Life Position to another. Nevertheless, the grid in Figure 5 provides a useful guide to what can be expected. It might seem surprising that the good qualities listed in the I'M OK – YOU'RE OK quarter of the grid could be thought of as Racket

I'M NOT OK – YOU'RE OK	I'M OK – YOU'RE OK
Scared	Joyful
Inferior	Loving
Unloved	Serene
Deprived	Kind
Helpless	Gentle
Guilty	Patient
Inadequate	Tolerant
Shy	Controlled
Defeated	Trustworthy
Embarrassed	
I'M NOT OK – YOU'RE NOT OK	**I'M OK – YOU'RE NOT OK**
Sad	Angry
Despairing	Jealous
Hopeless	Resentful
Pig sick	Bitter
Confused	Persecuted
Lost	Unappreciated
Isolated	Suspicious
Alone	Superior

Figure 5 Typical Racket Feelings

Feelings. This may be the case more frequently than some people suppose, however, though some practitioners might prefer to ascribe these Racket Feelings to one of the other Life Positions – possibly I'M NOT OK – YOU'RE OK.

The Pagliacci Syndrome

Every experienced therapist has met clients who manifest such good-humoured and gracious self-assurance that it is difficult to understand why they should seek the services of a therapist at all. It frequently transpires, however, that the person is covering up a seething cauldron of emotions such as anger, fear, or sadness which they have never been free to express. Their apparent joyfulness, serenity, or loving-kindness may be a carefully contrived defensive system that the therapist must dismantle, if at all, only with the greatest care and offering abundant protection (*see* Chapter 13). This phenomenon occurs so frequently that I have called it 'The Pagliacci Syndrome', recalling the Prologue to Act I of Leoncavallo's opera, *I Pagliacci* [The Clowns], in which the clown sings 'To act with my heart maddened with sorrow; I know not what I'm saying or what I'm doing. Yet I must face it! Courage, my heart! Thou art not a man, thou art but a jester!'

In the same sort of way, some people conceal their true feelings – perhaps even from themselves. They put on an act, with their hearts 'maddened with sorrow', or with fear or anger or even with a Racket Feeling which is, in itself, a cover-up for yet another Racket Feeling! The authentic feeling might be hidden beneath several layers, and to uncover it might be like peeling an onion. This can sometimes be done by asking the client what the feeling she is actually having *feels* like. For example:

THERAPIST: What is it like to feel so cheerful all the time when life is so fraught?

CLIENT: I feel much more in control.

THERAPIST: In control of what?

CLIENT: Everything. You can't let things get you down, can you?

THERAPIST: What is it that might get you down if you stopped to think about it?

CLIENT: Life ... Everything.

THERAPIST: What in particular?

CLIENT: Oh ... not being loved as a kid ... rejected ... exploited ... abused, I suppose.

THERAPIST: And what does it feel like to be abused?

CLIENT: Scary. You never know when it's going to happen again.

THERAPIST: Can you feel that fear now?

CLIENT: Of course I can.

THERAPIST: What does it feel like to feel scared?

CLIENT: I just feel ... helpless.

THERAPIST: And if you had all the power you need in order to not feel scared, what would you be able to feel then?

CLIENT: I don't know.

THERAPIST: Yes, you do. What would be a really useful feeling to have so that you could put a stop to the abuse and never feel scared again?

(At this point, as you get near to the heart of the matter, the client might begin to weep.)

THERAPIST: What would a useful feeling be?

CLIENT: I'd be bloody angry!
              (*Cathartic tears of rage might then follow, demanding
              further work leading to relief and resolution before the
              session is terminated.*)

While most Racket Feelings might be disagreeable and
unpleasant, however, they are nevertheless paradoxically comfortable
because they are so familiar – like the ticker-tape machine chattering
away in the corner of the office; and, if it stops, the staff can't settle
down to work until the engineer has come and repaired it. Similarly,
we tend to be our own 'engineers' and set up our own familiar Racket
Feelings. We can sometimes set up our Racket Feelings even without
a game-playing partner. Withdrawal is the most effective time-
structure for doing this. While withdrawn temporarily from the
reality of what is actually going on in the world (e.g., the lecturer
talking away in front of us while we switch from an Adult to a Child
ego state; or while we are driving the car on 'automatic pilot') we can
fantasize about imaginery bad experiences and provoke bad Racket
Feelings in ourselves as a result.

One of the objects of transactional analysis is to learn how to stop
setting up Racket Feelings and how to stop playing the psychological
Games that result in them and thereby advancing our Scripts.
Instead, we learn how to structure our time in ways that produce
positive Strokes, good feelings, and a sense of personal worth.

Racket System Analysis is an important area of transactional
analysis which was first introduced by Richard Erskine and Marilyn
Zalcman in 1979.[13] This therapeutic process is briefly summarized in
Chapter 13.

7 Life Positions

For thousands of years people have believed that human beings could be divided into four basic types according to their temperaments. The ancient Greeks called them Sanguine, Melancholic, Choleric, and Phlegmatic. It might be, of course, that these dispositions, like extroversion and introversion, are at least partly determined genetically. But even that does not mean that they are fixed and unchangeable.

The diagram of the Life Positions grid in Figure 6 draws together a lot of information, and you might like to refer to it as you read the following paragraphs.

The Sanguine person is cheerful, optimistic, and realistic, and expects things to go well. He is in charge of his own life and can GET ON WITH people and with life in general. In TA we describe this position as I'm OK – You're OK or, to give it in full, I'm OK for me – You're OK for me. When we are in this Life Position we are not indulging in Rackets, not experiencing Racket Feelings, not playing Games, and not functioning from a Destructive (P1 or C1) Child ego state. We can engage in problem solving and negotiating, and we can enjoy life. No 'escape' from this position is necessary. It should be remembered, however, that the 'good feelings' in the top right-hand corner of the Typical Racket Feelings grid in Figure 5 can, in some circumstances, be substitutes for such problem-solving feelings as Anger, Fear, or Sadness, described in the last chapter as suggesting 'The Pagliacci Syndrome'.

The Melancholic person is in the Depressive Position. He or she is likely to be pessimistic and gloomy, and the characteristic attitude is (briefly) I'm not OK – You're OK. They might feel Fear as a Racket Feeling but it will be unfruitful if there is nothing in present reality to be scared of or to get away from. The Adapted Child (P1) stance of someone in the Depressive Position is likely to be Helpless and he will probably start Game-playing from the Victim role; but sometimes he might start as Rescuer because of his inclination towards appeasing, conciliating, and deferring to others. His deep desire is to want to Get Away From people and problems. If he gets too deeply into this mood he might even try to get away from life altogether by attempting suicide

I'm Not OK (for me) (– +) – You're OK (for me)	I'm OK (for me) (+ +) – You're OK (for me)
MELANCHOLIC	**SANGUINE**
DEPRESSIVE POSITION	IN CHARGE OF LIFE
Style – GET AWAY FROM	Style – GET ON WITH
Disposition – DEPRESSED	Disposition – OPTIMISTIC/JOYFUL
Racket Feeling – FEAR	Racket Feeling – NONE
Game Starting Position – RESCUER or VICTIM	Game Starting Position – NONE
Adapted Child Stance – HELPLESS or HELPFUL	Adapted Child Stance – NONE
Activities – APPEASING CONCILIATING ADAPTING	Activities – PROBLEM SOLVING NEGOTIATING ENJOYMENT
Escape Hatch – SUICIDE	Escape Hatch – NONE (unnecessary)
I'm Not OK (for me) (– –) – You're Not OK (for me)	I'm OK (for me) (+ –) – You're Not OK (for me)
PHLEGMATIC	**CHOLERIC**
SCHIZOID POSITION	PARANOID POSITION
Style – GET NOWHERE WITH	Style – GET RID OF
Disposition – PESSIMISTIC	Disposition – CRITICAL
Racket Feeling – SADNESS	Racket Feeling – ANGER
Game Starting Position – VICTIM	Game Starting Position – PERSECUTOR
Adapted Child Stance – HELPLESS or HURTFUL	Adapted Child Stance – HURTFUL or HELPFUL
Activities – DOING NOTHING AVOIDANCE SABOTAGE	Activities – CONTROLLING CRITICIZING TAKING CARE OF
Escape Hatch – PSYCHOSIS	Escape Hatch – HOMICIDE

Figure 6   Life Positions Grid

as an escape from the responsibility for solving problems. Suicide becomes, in that event, his 'escape hatch'.

The Choleric person is in the Paranoid Position. He is often angry and tends to blame others rather than himself for anything that goes wrong. His attitude is summed up in the expression I'm OK – You're Not OK and his desire is often to Get Rid Of whoever it is he blames for life's disasters – a person, perhaps, or a subculture, or the government of the day! Criminals often fall into this category. They might be oversensitive in the face of criticism but be highly critical of others and have a tendency to get angry when there is nothing in reality that calls for anger and nothing that anger can change. The anger then is 'rackety'. They like to be in control of people and might aim to achieve control by being either Hurtful or Helpful. Police officers and social workers, for example, sometimes function from this Life Position. Anyone who gets too deeply into the Choleric, Paranoid, or I'm OK – You're Not OK Life Position might be at risk of Getting Rid Of the Not-OK people altogether, perhaps by locking them up or even by killing them! For them Homicide might be an escape hatch or cop-out from the responsibility for solving problems.

A person in the I'm Not OK – You're Not OK Life Position tends to be Phlegmatic and Schizoid. This is in many respects the worst Life Position of all because it seems to the person that there is no one who can help. Such people feel as if they can Get Nowhere With either people or life in general, and they tend to become very isolated and withdrawn. They develop a despairing disposition, feel rackety sadness when they have suffered no particular loss, and are likely to get into the Victim position at the start of a psychological Game, probably switching to Persecutor. The Adapted Child stance is usually Helpless or Hurtful, and their whole life's course is often characterized by avoidance, sabotaging any possible achievement, or simply doing nothing. If they get too deeply into this Life Position they might 'go crazy'. At its worst the 'going Crazy' Escape Hatch can mean becoming psychotic and cutting off from reality altogether which, in some cases, could issue in either suicide or homicide. More frequently, it means some kind of 'nervous breakdown' which falls short of psychosis; either way it provides an escape from the responsibility for solving problems and someone else has to take over.

Closing Escape Hatches

These extreme reactions we call 'Escape Hatches' because they are all ways in which people might seek to escape from the responsibility for solving problems. Sometimes people who are in therapy might want to cop out from that responsibility because the therapeutic process, which requires them to face up to reality, becomes too painful. One way to protect them from this is to ask them to close their escape hatches. This procedure is dealt with in Chapter 13 on Practical Counselling.

When the Going Gets Rough

Most people spend *some* time in each of the Life Positions. But we all have a tendency (because of our particular personality type) to take refuge in a particular one of the Not OK positions when the going gets rough. It is important in therapy to identify which Life Position the client is most likely to slip into in such circumstances. This will say a great deal about the client's expectations of himself and the general direction of his Script or Life Plan, including the Racket Feelings he is likely to experience most readily to advance his Script.

A goal of transactional analysis is to spend as much time as possible in the I'm OK – You're OK Life Position where we can Get on With people and Get on With life. Of course, we all slip out of this OK position from time to time when the stresses of life build up, but we discover, through the process of therapy, that we do not need to wait until 'things' change, or until the storm blows itself out, before we can resume an OK Life Position. We can in principle (though it might demand a lot of therapy in practice) simply *decide* to live with the belief and attitude 'I'm OK – You're OK'. We can then be in charge of our own lives.

You will note that, in the centre of the Life Positions grid (Figure 6) there are crossed arrows. These are to indicate that those whose 'favourite' Life Position is, for example, I'm Not OK – You're OK might tend to flip over from time to time into the I'm OK – You're Not OK Life Position and vice versa. And someone who slips most readily into the I'm Not OK – You're Not OK Life Position when the going gets rough might, surprisingly, flip into it from I'm OK – You're OK when the going is particularly congenial! A curious phenomenon is the tendency of some people to flip into one of the Not-OK Life Positions soon after achieving some goal they have long strived for – perhaps getting a good degree or becoming a parent.

Personality Adaptations

In addition to our Life Positions, human beings tend to make fairly clearly defined adaptations when very young in response to the Script Messages (Injunctions, Counter-injunctions, Drivers, Permissions, and Programme) we receive from parents and other significant grown-ups. Six basic Personality Adaptations identified by Paul Ware[14] are Schizoid, Hysterical, Obsessive-Compulsive, Paranoid, Antisocial, and Passive-Aggressive. The use of these adaptations in therapy is dealt with by Ian Stewart in *Developing TA Counselling*.[15]

8 The Script Against *Physis*

The Script is a life plan established in the early years of childhood, and is a deviation from 'what might have been'. By the time a child is six years old, he or she has well-established (even though unconscious) expectations about the direction life will take. In the light of early experiences of living in a world of giants, the youngster has to work out what is the best way to survive. His decision is, as Woollams and Brown say, 'a compromise between his wants, on the one hand, and his vulnerability to outside pressures on the other hand'.[16] It is the Little Professor (A1 or Adult-in-the-Child) who makes these Early Decisions, guided mainly by intuition, feelings, and fragments of information picked up subliminally when, being very small, he has not much to go on in the way of hard facts. During the following few years, reinforcing experiences help to fill in the details.

The two diagrams in Figure 7 on p. 47 are based on Script Matrix diagrams that appear in the standard literature but both include, in addition, the 'Arrow of Aspiration' representing *Physis* which is dealt with in this chapter. Both diagrams show the kind of messages from Mother and Father that lead to the youngster's Early Decisions and contribute to the Script or Life Plan. The descriptions attached to the messages in the two diagrams appear to be different; the reader will find on studying them, however, that they are really the same but put in different words to clarify what is happening. Figure 7(a) (based on a diagram by Woollams and Brown)[16] I regard as more appropriate when considering basic Script formation, because it shows all the messages from Mother and Father being received into the youngster's Child ego state where the foundations of the Script are, in fact, established very early in life.

But there is more to a Script than its foundations; there are a lot of details to be filled in later and a good deal of reinforcement takes place as a result of life experiences. Sometimes these experiences seem to 'bear out', and therefore reinforce, the Early Decisions made when the youngster did not understand what was really going on and why. For example, a very small child might make an Early Decision at the age of two, to the effect that 'I am worthless and my

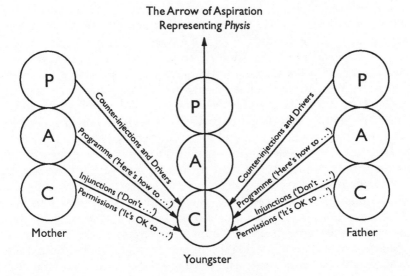

Figure 7(a) The Script Against *Physis*

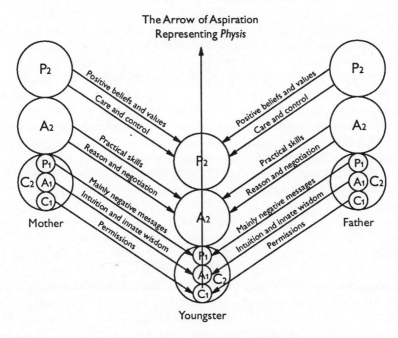

Figure 7(b) The Script Against *Physis*

Mummy doesn't love me', as the result of his mother having been taken into hospital for major surgery and the youngster put in the care of grandparents. He is wrong about the facts (his Mother does love him, really) but if, when he is eight years old, his mother leaves home because her husband is ill-treating her and the youngster finishes up with his grandparents yet again, then the original Early Decision, though based on a misunderstanding of the facts, is likely to be reinforced. This Early Decision might then lay the foundations for serious pathology, perhaps depression, much later in life. Figure 7(b) – which is the one most commonly used in TA books – is better for considering the way in which the youngster's Script is reinforced as life goes on and for taking into account the way in which his Adult ego state is developed as he learns all kinds of practical skills and is educated in reason and in social relationships. And, of course, it is easier to see from Figure 7(b) and its descriptions, how the growth of the youngster's character depends on his receiving sound moral guidance in the way of beliefs and values, which will be important when we come to consider character disorder in Chapters 11 and 12.

It will be seen from both diagrams that mainly negative messages come from the Child ego state in Mother and Father. These messages do not represent the parents' natural and wholesome desires for their youngster (which would come from P2 or Creative C1) but from their *adapted* desires in P1, which have sometimes been passed on from *their* parents – like a 'hot potato'.[17] These 'second-order' elements in the Child ego state are familiar from the New Ego State Model and should be assumed as present also in Figure 7(a). Chapter 2 has shown that positive messages (particularly encouragements to empathize and to be sensitive to the feelings of others) might also come from this source (P1); and we saw that Permissions coming from the Natural child (C1) in Mother and Father, might sometimes actually give their youngster *carte blanche* for quite antisocial behaviour and contribute to some very negative scripting.

A disturbing example of such toxic permission occurred in front of the television cameras in the mid-1990s when riots were taking place on a housing estate in the north-east of England. Two youths crashed a car into a lamp-post and were killed. The media referred to them as 'joy riders' and the father of one of them was outraged. He declared before the cameras: 'My lad was no joy rider. He was a professional criminal. That was the get-away car'! There can be little room for doubt that that father's antisocial attitude had effectively been giving his son permission to commit crime probably since the lad was born.

Winners, Losers, and Non-winners

Some people establish life plans that provide for a good deal of happiness and personal success; they evidently have charge of their own lives. But all too often we hear of eminent people who have succeeded in politics, business, films, or theatre, for example, but whose private lives might be dogged by alcoholism, drug addiction, sexual difficulties, failed marriages, depression, or some other emotional distress. In one respect they are Winners, but in other areas of life – perhaps far more important to ultimate human happiness – they are Losers.

Real Winners collect Positive Strokes and give plenty of Positive Strokes to other people. Most of them are probably quite ordinary folk of no great public consequence, secure in their families and happy in their jobs but not newsworthy, so we hear nothing about them. They have just quietly discovered the secret of living. Their Life Position can be summed up in the expression 'I'm OK – You're OK'.

Losers have learned from infancy that life will not go well for them. They have been brought up on a diet of Negative Strokes and rackety bad feelings. They collect these bad feelings and save them up until they have enough to justify some really bad experience, such as a serious breakdown in relationships, a suicide, a prison sentence, a mental illness, or death from some cause that could have been avoided – alcohol poisoning, for example.

Of course, everybody makes mistakes. But Winners learn how to prevent the same mistake happening repeatedly and Losers learn how to make such mistakes – or perhaps some new ones – happen over and over again. Winners know what they will do next if they lose (which we all do sometimes); Losers just imagine what they will do if they win.

But many people – in fact, the overwhelming majority – are neither Winners nor Losers but merely Non-winners. Non-winners learn how to survive on a mixture of Positive and Negative Strokes. Life for them is not so much a tragedy as a disappointment. Things could have been so much better if only they had acted differently at some important stage in life.

This life plan is called a Script because it is in many respects like the script of a play. The player performs it almost as an actor plays a part on the stage, although he is not aware of the significance of what he is doing. He will attract to himself other players to fill important roles, marry them or work with them, or just make friends with them – or enemies, perhaps – and will unconsciously manipulate them to produce for himself the 'Script Pay-off' which, in his heart of hearts, he always 'knew' would happen because 'life's like that'.

Scripts, like plays, are written to be replayed repeatedly. The curtain comes down at the end but the next night the players will return, go back on stage, say the same lines, and do the same things all over again. For many unhappy people marriage is like that! Some of the actors playing the parts might change but the same old story line repeats itself.

Early Decisions

Scripts are based on Early Decisions made when we were too young to understand what was really going on. One example quoted earlier was of a youngster whose mother went into hospital for surgery and the child thought she had deserted him. Another example is of a youngster who decides, 'I'll keep out of everybody's way so that I don't annoy them and then they won't reject me'. Hearing Mother or Father say, 'Don't you be angry with me', the Little Professor (not knowing that Dad has just lost his job and is upset) asks, 'How am I going to handle this?' He then makes a wise decision such as 'I'll nurse my anger in secret' – which ensures that he is not entirely rejected, as he imagines he would be if he expressed his anger openly.

Such decisions, once made, are likely to continue into adult life so that when the person is twenty-five or sixty he is not free to be, say, authentically angry when a burst of anger might have been exactly the right way to solve a problem. Or he cannot grieve with authentic sadness when he has really suffered loss. With the understanding and insight gained in transactional analysis such an Early Decision can be changed in the light of here and now reality and afterwards life can take off in a new direction.

Injunctions and Permissions

These Early Decisions are made in response to 'messages' received from parents and other authority figures in childhood, as indicated on the Script Matrix diagrams in Figure 7. The messages include Permissions and Injunctions. The Permissions are (usually) positive messages from Mother or Father, allowing the youngster to grow and develop and to be creative and adventurous. The Injunctions, however, are essentially 'Don't ...' messages received non-verbally from the Parent-in-the-Child ego state of Mother or Father. Later they might be reinforced verbally but, to begin with, an Injunction is received when the youngster picks up intuitively what the parents want or need *for themselves*. The child's interests are not the primary consideration. *It is parental self-interest that provides the motivation for these inhibiting messages and restricts the youngster's freedom to be his authentic self.*

The following is a list of the twelve basic Injunctions developed by Bob and Mary Goulding.[18]

Don't exist	Don't succeed	Don't ...!
Don't be you	Don't be important	Don't be well (or sane)
Don't be a child	Don't belong	Don't think
Don't grow up	Don't be close	Don't feel

An illustration might help to explain how Injunctions develop. Within moments of birth, and perhaps even sooner, a baby can sense intuitively whether she is welcome in the world and enjoys Mother's unconditional love. The manner in which Mother holds her, the tone of Mother's voice, and many other factors even more subtle, can convey to a new-born child that she is, or is not, really wanted. Later, when she is a year or two old and playing in the kitchen whilst Mother is baking or preparing a meal, she might hear Mother say irritably, 'Get out from under my feet, will you! Go and play somewhere else.' A few messages like this, delivered with good humour and accompanied by an abundance of affection and plenty of Positive Strokes, will not be damaging to the youngster; but if they continue and are unaccompanied by the encouraging nurture and Permissions every child needs for normal growth and development, the youngster might begin to think, 'My Mummy doesn't love me'. Or even, 'My Mummy will never be happy as long as I'm here'. And if, at a later date, she hears her Mother saying conversationally to a visiting friend, 'If it hadn't been for *her* I would have gone to medical school', then she might begin to wonder whether Mother really wants her to be dead! Although her Mother never actually said, 'Drop dead!', the child might nevertheless receive a very powerful 'Don't exist' message. In extreme cases, if this is reinforced by later life experiences, it could even lead to suicide!

Other Injunctions develop in a similar sort of way and some, of course, will be more intense or powerful than others in terms of their effect on the youngster's Script.

Counter-injunctions and Drivers

Also received are Counter-injunctions from the Parent ego state of Mother or Father, which are usually benign and constructive in nature and intent. They carry useful guidelines for living such as

'Always tell the truth', 'Work hard', 'Treat people with respect', or 'Wear the right clothes on the right occasion', and a whole host of proverbs and wise sayings that have been passed down the generations for hundreds of years. However, some Counter-injunctions, called Drivers (of which only five have been identified), can be toxic and destructive in terms of the youngster's personal development.

The following are the five Drivers identified by Taibi Kahler and his co-workers:[19, 20]

Be perfect   Be strong   Please me (or someone)
          Try hard   Hurry up

A Driver comes from the Parent ego state of the parents and *drives* the youngster into a certain kind of behaviour by putting a condition on his sense of personal worth. While Drivers and other Counter-injunctions are usually shown as being received into the youngster's Parent ego state (P2), as in Figure 7(b), some Script Matrix diagrams, such as Figure 7(a), show the messages going to the youngster's Child ego state (P1), where the Script is formed. So, while Counter-injunctions in general (conveying good moral and social guidance) are received into the youngster's Parent ego state (P2), it should be noted that messages delivered early in life are also received into the youngster's Parent-in-the-Child ego state (P1), featured in Figure 7(b). These Driver messages are, in general, less potent than the messages from the parents' Child ego states because they are less emotionally charged, but they are nevertheless significant and they provide material for what is best called the Subscript. The term 'counterscript' has sometimes been used but this suggests that it is in opposition to the Script and that is not necessarily so. As Woollams and Brown say, 'The subscript includes a lifestyle that is not only closely connected to the script, but is also a part of the process of carrying out the script.'[16]

Even those five special Counter-injunctions we call Drivers will probably be intended by Mother or Father or other parent figure to be nurturing and encouraging of the child's growing maturity. Because the Drivers put a condition on the youngster's sense of OK-ness, however, they can become seriously toxic and might also carry an Injunction. For example, the Driver 'Try hard' tells the youngster he is OK *only if* he is trying hard. But 'Try hard', especially if delivered urgently, might carry with it an implicit message that the youngster is not really expected to succeed; this can then amount to a 'Don't succeed' Injunction. So he is in a double-bind because the effort itself is counter-productive. 'Be strong' can carry the Injunction 'Don't have (or don't express) feelings'; 'Be perfect' (an impossible task!) carries the Injunction 'Don't make it' or 'Don't succeed'. 'Please me (or someone)' might also mean 'Don't be your true self; please me instead'. 'Hurry up' can also result in an Injunction 'Don't think'. For example, a man is hurriedly packing for a sudden and unexpected trip abroad and in his rush to deal with important domestic contingencies he might forget to take his electric shaver – or even his passport! It is common experience that when we are in a hurry we don't pay proper attention or we forget things.

Process Therapy, developed by Taibi Kahler, makes particular use of the concept of Drivers in relation to the Mini-script. This is a sequence of scripty behaviours, beliefs, and feelings which might be experienced within a few minutes, or even seconds, and during that short period it reproduces and reinforces the process of the entire Life Script.[19, 20] There is further brief reference to Process Therapy in Chapter 13. A more detailed account of this therapeutic approach is provided by Ian Stewart and Vann Joines in Chapter 16 of *TA To-Day*.[21]

The Programme

Messages from the Adult ego state of Mother or Father to the Adult ego state of the youngster are called The Programme. The import of these messages is summed up in the words 'Here's how to ...', as in Figure 7(a). They comprise Adult guidance, as indicated in Figure 7(b), on the development of practical skills such as studying for an exam, sailing a dinghy, or learning language, for example, as well as the development of reason and negotiating ability.

Physis

Before he began to write about transactional analysis, Eric Berne published *The Layman's Guide to Psychiatry and Psychoanalysis*[22] in which he introduced the concept of the Parent, Adult, and Child ego states. 'But', he observed, 'there is something beyond this – some force which drives people to grow, progress and do better.' He found an answer to this in the work of the Oxford Greek scholar, Gilbert Murray, who had written of the ancient notion of '*Physis*, the growth force of Nature, which eternally strives to make things grow and to make growing things more perfect'. Berne concluded that 'the growth force, or *Physis*, which we see evidence of in the individual and society, if properly nourished in infancy, works along with the Superego, so that the individual has an urge to grow and to behave "better" – that is, in accordance with principles which take the happiness of others into consideration'.

It is important to note Berne's observation that *Physis* needs to be 'properly nourished in infancy' if it is to emerge as an effective growth force in human personality. The necessary nourishment is provided by the parents of the infant from their entire personalities, including their own Parent ego states, ensuring the Care and Control emphasized in Chapter 2 as essential for healthy growth and development. A horticultural analogy will make sense to every gardener: a daffodil bulb must be planted in fertile soil if the life invested in it is to emerge as a flower; and it must also be watered. Similarly, the infant human being must be planted in fertile 'social soil' and be 'watered' with abundant human love and affection, Care and Control, if he is to emerge as a 'total human being', as described in Part 3 of this book. And a social environment which encourages and supports the parents themselves is also necessary for optimum growth of the infant.

When Berne wrote about the development of the Script, or life plan, in his last book, *What Do You Say After You Say Hello?*[5] he included in one of his Script Matrix diagrams the Arrow of Aspiration, which is featured in both diagrams in Figure 7, indicating the upward thrust towards perfection that life would follow if the infant was well nourished and progress was not interfered with. Petruska Clarkson, to whom we owe the rediscovery of *Physis*, has said that the Arrow of Aspiration 'corresponds pictorially with the philosophical concept of *Physis*'; and she sees in Berne's diagram 'one of the most powerful images in TA literature of the potential of human beings to liberate themselves from the deterministic constraints of their scripts'.[23] Clarkson writes more fully about *Physis* in her book for advanced practitioners, *Transactional Analysis Psychotherapy – an Integrated Approach.*[24]

The Arrow of Aspiration, representing *Physis*, thrusts upwards from the Child ego state (C1) in the direction of growth, creativity, and personal fulfilment. Wholesome messages from the Parent ego states of Mother and Father (or their later substitutes) when received into the Parent ego state of the youngster, provide the primary element in the nurture which it is essential for *Physis* to receive to fuel its drive towards fulfilment and, ideally, perfection. But the Script arrows, representing messages from Mother, Father, and others (which, despite the Permissions and Parent nurture, are often, on balance, toxic) can be seen as thrusting downwards in opposition. The term 'Script Proper' is sometimes used to refer to the whole complex of Injunctions, Permissions, Counter-injunctions, Drivers, and Programme together with the Early Decisions based on them.

This brief account of how the Script is established and how it functions provides a background to understanding how our Scripts impede us in becoming what we really are. Script Analysis is an element in transactional analysis psychotherapy which is concerned with discovering what are these impediments to personal growth and fulfilment and then taking therapeutic steps to overcome or eliminate them, so that the person can respond to his personal *Physis* and begin to achieve his real potential. Counsellors who wish to include Script Analysis as a part of the therapeutic process will, of course, need to explore this area in much more depth.

9 How People Avoid Solving Problems

Jacqui Lee Schiff, a social worker, was one of Eric Berne's early associates. She developed a radical new way of treating young schizophrenics by adopting them into her own family and effectively bringing them up all over again. Her work is described in the book *All My Children*.[25] Jacqui Schiff's approach was politically contentious, involving, in some cases, fully supported regression in which a young adult might 'become little' for a prolonged period and be re-parented by therapists who took the role of parents, each developmental stage taking from three to six weeks. This rarely, if ever, happens today. Nevertheless, treatment, in a residential setting, might take several years in some cases, and this is being developed in several countries, including Britain, for the treatment of schizophrenia, eating disorders, and other severe mental illnesses. The theoretical basis for the therapeutic programme is described in *Cathexis Reader*.[26] The general principles, however, are applicable to a wide range of conditions of a far less serious nature. There is a very brief account in Chapter 13 of the principles behind the Cathexis approach to treating severe mental illness.

The basic assumption, from which Jacqui Schiff and her co-workers began, was that people behave as they do because they choose to do so, rather than because they can't help it. Treatment, therefore, starts from the belief that the individual has within himself the resources necessary to accomplish his own recovery, a view that is consistent with Berne's concept of *Physis*. She says:

> Operating on the assumption that a healthy organism is reactive, a major focus for research has been on how people *don't* do things or don't do them effectively. Passivity in thinking, feeling and doing disrupts the balance of social functioning and results in internal distress or behaviour disorders. We see passivity as resulting from unresolved dependency (symbiosis).[26]

Symbiosis means 'living together' in the sense of two people being emotionally dependent on each other. The condition, which occurs

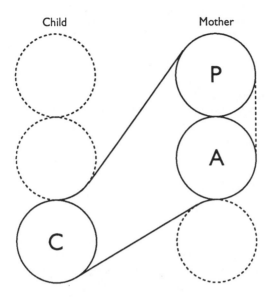

Figure 8 Symbiosis

naturally between mother and baby, is diagrammed as in Figure 8 above, which shows mother and baby as having a full set of ego states between them. In parenting, Mother has had to forego, temporarily, her Child ego state; she may not give any priority to meeting her own Child needs.

In the normal course of growing up, the child develops his own Adult and Parent ego states and no longer needs his mother to do his thinking for him or to care for and control him. The bond between mother and child then gradually breaks down and the Symbiosis is resolved. Where there is no satisfactory resolution, however, the youngster, as a grown-up person, is likely to continue seeking unconsciously for mother or a mother substitute. In that event, the continuing Symbiosis becomes pathological and might seriously interfere with mental health. The grown-up person might tend, in his Child ego state, to engage with another person's Parent ego state and to depend on the other person (as a substitute for Mother) to solve his problems for him. This condition is sometimes described as 'co-dependency', particularly if both parties get sucked into it. The consequence is Passivity – which might appear superficially to be very active but its essential characteristic is that it enables a person to *avoid solving the problem*. The responsibility for problem solving is then left to someone else – including a counsellor or therapist if she or he is not very careful!

It seems likely, however, that some benign residue of the original Symbiosis, the normal dependency between mother and baby, usually remains and this provides the basis for many healthy relationships of *agreed* mutual dependency, as in marriage. Perhaps this is why Barbra Streisand sang 'people who need people are the luckiest people in the world'! But perhaps it is not 'needing' people (which can be co-dependency and pathological) but *wanting* them and loving them sacrificially, as in good parenting, that provides the stimulus for psychological and spiritual growth – as we shall see in Chapter 14.

Transference and Counter-transference

'A working knowledge of symbiosis', say the Schiffs, 'enables a therapist to teach a patient how to function in problem-solving, to utilize the transference in the service of treatment goals, and to make rapid and crisp intervention in transactions.'[26] There are many ways of defining 'transference'. It is described by Rycroft as 'the process by which a patient displaces on to his analyst feelings, ideas, etc., which derive from previous figures in his life'.[27] Freud says, 'the patient sees in his analyst the return – the reincarnation – of some important figure out of his childhood or past, and consequently transfers on to him feelings and reactions that undoubtedly applied to this model'.[28] The recipients of such transferred thoughts, feelings, and behaviours are not, however, exclusively therapists of one sort or another, though therapists are especially vulnerable; such transference can sometimes occur with almost anyone who stands temporarily in a parent–child kind of relationship to another person, regardless of the social realities.

Counter-transference occurs when the therapist's emotional attitude to the client is in response to the patient's transference. This can be seen either as a distorting element in treatment or as clinical evidence of the client's true intentions or meaning.[27] For example, the father of a client I shall call Elaine was a doctor in an administrative appointment; he took a particularly detached and objective approach to his family as well as to his work. Elaine transferred her father's Adult 'face' on to me, perceiving me as detached and 'Adult' even though my natural disposition is to be warm and parental. I did not immediately realize what was going on but was able to recognize in supervision that I was actually adopting an uncharacteristically detached approach to Elaine which was quite unhelpful to the therapeutic process.

The Passive Behaviours

There are four 'passive behaviours' which people use in attempting to establish or maintain unhealthy symbiotic relationships. They are: Doing nothing, Over-adaptation, Agitation, and Incapacitation or Violence.

Doing nothing

This does not imply total inactivity but *doing nothing to solve the problem*. The person might be 'busy' doing all sorts of things that do not contribute to solving the problem!

Over-adaptation

The person who over-adapts does what he believes somebody else wants him to do, instead of working out a creative solution for himself. Over-adaptation is sometimes difficult to identify because it might be mistaken for a genuine creative adaptation, 'the client acting', as Clarkson says, '*as if* deep structural change has occurred'. Even so, 'overadaptation has the benefit of good thinking supporting it'.[24] It is, therefore, the easiest mode of Passivity for the therapist to work with because there is *some* movement, the person is usually amenable to treatment and discounting behaviour can be confronted.

Agitation

This involves repetitive behaviour that is not directed at any productive goal. Typical forms of Agitation are foot-tapping, nail-biting, chain-smoking, floor-pacing, and repetitive thinking in which the same thought goes round and round in the head. Agitation results from a build-up of energy for which there is no creative outlet, and it can be a sign of impending Violence or Incapacitation. Its significance, therefore, should not be underestimated.

The problem with Agitation is that anyone who has escalated to that level of passivity might find it extremely difficult, if not impossible, to cathect Adult without assistance. The therapist's best option is usually to use a very strong Parent voice, telling the client authoritatively to 'breathe deeply … count slowly up to ten … stand up and look around the room and tell me what you see … What books are on the top shelf? … Choose one you like and read the opening sentence … etc.'

In response to such instructions as these, the client will usually go first into Over-adaptation, from which mode of passivity it is easier for him to cathect Adult and get on to, or back on to, the therapeutic track. A married couple were in serious conflict over the wife's adultery. The husband was so enraged and distraught that he could not address the issues rationally at all but instead wept hysterically and banged his knee with his fist. He was quite Passive in problem solving and was Agitating dangerously. Accepting, for the moment, his child-like presentation of himself, I stood over him and, using his name, shouted at him to exercise self-control. I then used a Controlling Parent ego state to give him instructions such as those suggested above. The husband gradually responded and I was able to bring the session to a satisfactory conclusion.

Incapacitation or Violence

Both of these behaviours involve a failure to think and to solve problems, so that someone else (perhaps a doctor or a policeman) will have to take charge. Incapacitation might include becoming ill (backache is a popular illness of people who refuse to solve their financial problems by working when work is available), fainting (less fashionable now than in Victorian times), having a 'nervous break-down', or getting blind drunk. Violence needs no describing but it is a popular way of avoiding the responsibility for solving both marital problems and major political or international disputes!

Frame of Reference, Redefining and Discounting

Brief reference has already been made to these considerations in the chapter on the Analysis of Games. The 'frame of reference' is a way of perceiving the world which a youngster establishes in the early years of life and which is consistent with her Script or Life Plan. In a stressful situation later in life, when she has a problem to solve, she might then Redefine reality by leaving out of account, or Discounting, certain elements of what is actually going on in an attempt to make here and now fit her childhood perception of the world which is more comfortable by virtue of its familiarity. For example, if her childhood Script was built on the perception of herself as being inadequate in some way, she might, in grown-up stress, Discount – that is, leave out of account – her actual competence and ability to solve the problem in order to manipulate someone else into solving the problem for her. Hence, she becomes Passive.

The Schiffs and their co-workers observed that people might Discount in a variety of ways. They created a 'discounting matrix' to help in discovering which mode and type of discounting the client was using so that it could be confronted and 'detoxified'. This is presented in *Cathexis Reader*.[26]

Obviously, the use of the Cathexis Model with clients suffering from serious mental illnesses is a very specialized therapeutic field for advanced practitioners with specific training. For the reader's interest, however, the basic principles are outlined in Chapter 13.

Part Two:
Applied Transactional Analysis

10 Making a Contract

When we go to see the doctor with symptoms that are causing us distress, a few questions and a brief examination usually leads to a diagnosis and we are soon on the way to the pharmacist's with a prescription. Sometimes, of course, a visit to a consultant might be necessary but, in most cases, the direction of treatment is soon clear. People going to see a counsellor or psychotherapist, however, are often confused about what is the matter and what they want to do about it. They are like people setting off on a journey but they have no clear idea about where they want to get to; they simply don't like where they are at the moment! The first task, therefore, is to establish a therapeutic goal, otherwise they are most unlikely to arrive anywhere!

Sometimes it is possible to apply a diagnostic label and it is comforting, then, for both client and therapist to know 'where they are'. The use of *ICD 9* (the *International Classification of Diseases*)[29] or *DSM IV*, (the very comprehensive American *Diagnostic and Statistical Manual*)[30] can provide a basis for establishing a diagnosis and a treatment plan. This might sound daunting for those just exploring the possibilities of transactional analysis but, one way or another, client and therapist must agree about what they aim to do together.

A Therapeutic Partnership

One of the central features of transactional analysis is the establishment of a therapeutic partnership between counsellor or therapist and client with the object of achieving certain clearly defined goals. We call this Contracting. At the beginning, the Contract might be quite simply 'to find out about TA'. This would commit the therapist to some straightforward teaching and the client to a bit of reading between sessions. Soon, however, the client must consider what kind of changes he wants to make in the way he thinks, feels, and behaves – not the way *someone else* thinks, feels, and behaves!

The following are typical treatment contracts:

- to take a holiday and meet some new people;

- to set up home on my own;

- to reduce my weight by 2 stones in six months;

- to start training for the work I really want to do;

- to work regularly for a month, even when I don't really feel like it.

These are not promises of what the person will go ahead and do instantly; they are decisions by the client to reach a clear, observable objective in the course of therapy. Without such an observable goal there is no way of knowing that the presenting problem of, say, 'lack of confidence' or even 'agoraphobia' has been overcome. A great deal of work, over weeks, months, or even years, might be necessary before the goal is achieved. But both client and therapist know what they are aiming for and, once that is agreed, they can set out in the direction of their goal.

Actually deciding, or discovering, what that goal is to be, is frequently the most challenging part of the therapeutic process and, when agreed, it is often a considerable relief to therapist and to client. They are 'on track'. Frequently, people want to *stop* doing something, like drinking or gambling excessively, or having panic attacks or being depressed. But there is rarely any future in 'stop contracts', although stopping some self-destructive behaviour is frequently a means to a constructive end. For example, if someone wants to be physically fit so they can take part in competitive athletics, they might have to stop smoking, and stop overindulging in fattening foods! But the therapeutic contract is usually much more potent if it is about starting, rather than stopping, something.

The work during the session will then be about defining areas for change, that are currently subject to Script prohibitions, and then beginning to make those changes in the relatively safe environment of the counselling room and the therapeutic relationship. Bob and Mary Goulding would often start a therapy session by asking the client 'What do you want to change today?' They would then aim to facilitate an observable change within a few minutes. For example, a client who was unable to express anger would contract to express it and might do so in a session of cushion bashing! I have watched someone who was afraid of heights begin to overcome their phobia by climbing a ladder on to a garage roof during the therapy session.

Psychotherapy, however, is like physiotherapy in that the client must continue to work at his goals between therapy sessions if he is to gain optimum benefit. So he will frequently be asked by the therapist to do 'homework'. The same expectation might apply in counselling.

In addition to goals for significant life changes, therefore, the client will, ideally, make a clear and explicit agreement with the therapist or counsellor in respect of every piece of work done during a therapy session and for homework between sessions. This principle, however, should not be applied so inflexibly that it interferes with the all-important relationship between therapist and client, without which nothing useful is likely to take place. Nevertheless, it is important that counsellor and client know precisely what they are doing and why they are doing it. And the client is expected, in the terms of his contract, to invest energy in achieving his agreed goals.

Making a Contract

The first thing to be considered is the 'business contract'. This is based on sound commercial principles: (1) that the client is competent (in terms of age and understanding, etc.) to enter into a contract and that the therapist is competent to offer the kind of treatment needed; (2) that both parties agree about what they are aiming to do together; (3) that there is some agreed method of payment for services rendered; and (4) that the terms of the contract are legal and ethical.[4] These having been established, consideration can then be given to a therapeutic contract.

The following questions, addressed either to ourselves or, if we are therapists, to our clients, should help in arriving at a decision about what observable change is really being aimed for:

1 What is really bothering you about the way your life is going?

2 What do you want to change in *yourself*? (If others are behaving badly towards you, consider how you might be provoking them and think about changing that.)

3 Is this change something you sincerely desire for yourself and not just something you feel you *ought* to change?

4 Is the change you are proposing to make something new and not merely something you are already doing? (If you have already started on the way to your desired goal, what has so far prevented you from achieving it?)

5   Does the change you want to make affect all three dimensions of experience – thinking, feeling, and behaviour? (A Contract to *feel* different, while the client's thinking and behaviour remain unchanged, is unlikely to be successful.)

6   Is your goal realistic and practical, bearing in mind your physical, mental, and other resources? What does your common sense Adult ego state have to say about it? (For example, the client is not likely to make it as a professional footballer if he has only one leg! He should not be too easily discouraged, however: Evelyn Glennie became a professional musician of international stature despite being stone deaf!)

7   By what date do you aim to achieve your goal? (If the Contract does not have a completion date on it, it might go on and on and never see completion. Nevertheless, remember that Contracts are re-negotiable and can be extended if necessary. But a target date is important.)

8   Are you aiming to *do* something, not just to *stop* doing something?

9   What effect is your proposed change likely to have on other important people? (This might not always be a major consideration but the client's Parent ego state, recognizing his responsibilities for, say, his children or his partner, might need to approve his proposal. (Two-chair work, as described in Chapter 13, is one way to address this.)

10 Now ask the client to write down his proposed contract, possibly on the board if you are using one; but also record it on your case notes.

Finally, with the client, check the proposed Contract against the following criteria:

1   Is it a Contract to *start* doing something new, and not just a 'stop contract'?

2   Is it expressed in simple language an intelligent child could understand?

3   Can the client's goal be perceived and measured objectively by other people, including yourself as the counsellor?

4   Is what the client has written down declared from his unconta-
    minated Adult ego state? (Does it mean the same to other
    people, including you, as it means to the client?)

If the client's proposed Contract stands up to these tests, then he has
probably found a new direction in life and can begin to make his way
towards his goal, in partnership with you.

Particular care should be taken when making Contracts with
children whose parents are paying the counsellor's fee. The same
caution applies when the client, of whatever age, is being funded by
an agency such as the NHS, perhaps through a GP surgery, a
Department of Social Services, a private referral agency (of which
there are now several acting on behalf of industry and public
services), or by someone who might have an investment in the
outcome. In situations like this I usually insist – although not always
initially – that the client pays a part of my fee or gives some clear
evidence of genuine motivation.

From time to time I have been approached by friends or neighbours seeking professional help. As a general rule, I avoid entering
into a therapeutic Contract for on-going work in this situation. This
does not necessarily mean declining help altogether. I might discuss
the problem quite informally – and without payment, of course – and
then refer the person on to a suitably qualified colleague. It is wise to
be cautious, I feel, in working with anyone with whom the counsellor
has an on-going personal relationship, say in a club, church,
business, or any other setting in which the relationship will outlast
any professional Contract.

This issue also raises the matter of 'dual relationships' in the
context of counsellor training. The question arises whether it is
appropriate to be under Contract with the same person for, say,
training and supervision or for supervision and also for personal
therapy. In the early days of transactional analysis such dual relationships were taken for granted but, as counsellors and
psychotherapists seek recognized professional status, the matter of
such dual relationships is being widely discussed. Our own professional associations give guidance but the situation is still somewhat
fluid and not always easy to resolve, especially for those working in
some isolation. Each of us must address the issue as it arises and
discuss it with colleagues, especially supervisors.

11 Character Disorder – the Flip Side of Neurosis

General Considerations

The term 'character disorder' is used here in a distinctively transactional analysis sense. It refers to a condition in which the Parent ego state is either minimal or deviant, or even, in some cases, perhaps, missing entirely. In the 1960s, when transactional analysis was first introduced, most referrals to counsellors presented with anxiety states, depression, or phobias of one sort or another or, perhaps, with relationship problems. The focus of therapeutic interest was commonly the Child ego state, in particular the Adapted Child which is associated with the Parent-in-the-Child – P1 on the New Ego State Model. This ego state was generally believed to be adapting to oppressive parenting from Mother or Father, particularly in the 1960s when liberation from imposed traditional restraints, and the emotional distress associated with them, was a primary goal of therapy.

Clarkson has observed that 'In the permissive 60s a psychological refutation of oppressive collective Parent messages afforded a necessary and important rebalancing for our society. However, as new and more liberating permissive ethics have become part of our consciousness and clinical practice, there has often been another kind of imbalance.'[31] This, I believe, has resulted in an increase in referrals to counsellors of character-disordered clients, often second- or even third-generation people whose parenting has been permissive rather than oppressive and who lack, therefore, any clear moral guidelines. This is not only with regard to sexual behaviour but also the abuse of power, disregard for the law, the escalation in violence in the family, an increasing disposition to defraud the State by false claims for benefits of one kind and another, and many other infringements of moral and social mores which, a generation or two ago, would have been exceptional rather than commonplace. More and more children grow up in an environment of social and emotional instability because an increasing number of parents do not stay lovingly together long enough to provide it for them. In this situation *Physis*, the growth force of nature, described in Chapter 8, is frequently not nurtured with adequate care and control, and the condition referred to here as character disorder tends to develop.

My own awareness of character disorder as a seriously disabling condition arose from twenty-five years in the Probation Service, during which it was my responsibility to help law-breakers prove (which is what 'probation' means) that they could lead law-abiding lives. Character disorder is an extraordinarily difficult condition to discuss because, inescapably, it deals with moral behaviour – which has come to be regarded as an entirely private matter. In fact, there is a widely held belief, which counsellors and those in allied professions adhere to with particular tenacity, that 'Thou shalt not commit a value judgement'.[32] Antisocial behaviour is commonly attributed to the state of society and blamed on the politicians. Whether or not this is just, the counsellor, caseworker, psychotherapist, probation officer, or some other helping person, is left 'holding the baby' and is virtually prohibited by current philosophy from addressing amoral or immoral behaviour at all, even when it is clearly the manifest cause of the client's problem. Criminal behaviour is only the tip of the iceberg. Just as schizophrenia is rarely diagnosed in the absence of gross and bizarre mental disturbances, so character disorder is rarely acknowledged unless the person's behaviour is so antisocial as to be frankly criminal – and only a court of law has the right to make a judgement about that! So, in the counselling room, character disorder might go unacknowledged, undiagnosed, and untreated. But it is a very real and socially disabling condition that often leads to unfruitful conflict, broken relationships (whether with individuals or with society in general), and consequent emotional distress, such as depression and anxiety, *even when the person is generally law abiding*.

Transactional analyst Mavis Klein has contrasted 'character' with 'personality and temperament which', she says, 'is largely innate'. But character 'is wholly formed by instructions. It refers to entrenched beliefs about what is moral and "good" and what is immoral and "bad", which beliefs and values direct us in nurturing and controlling ourselves as well as others ... Children internalise the values given them by their parents.'[33] I would add to Klein's observations only that the 'instructions' by which character is formed are conveyed as much by example as by verbal teaching.

Scott Peck[34] makes the concept of responsibility the criterion for determining whether a person is neurotic or character disordered. 'The neurotic', he says, 'assumes too much responsibility, the person with a character disorder not enough.' The distinction is oversimplified but, in my view, useful in the early stages of diagnosis. He adds,

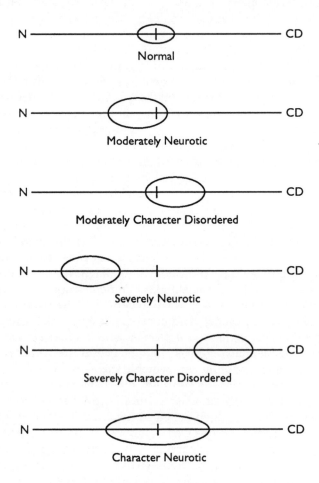

Figure 9 The Neurosis–Character Disorder Continuum

'Those with character disorders are much more difficult, if not impossible, to work with because they don't see themselves as the source of their problems'. But, as with any other condition, not all character disorders are equally severe, and the majority are not criminals. Also, many clients are 'character neurotic', manifesting features of character disorder and of neurosis. So there are some it is possible to help.

The Neurosis–Character Disorder Continuum in Figure 9 (opposite) is a diagrammatic way of representing the relative severity of neurosis or character disorder or, alternatively, the diagnosis of character-neurotic.

Sorting Out the Labels

Psychopathic personality, sociopath, antisocial personality, character disorder – these are only a few of the terms used to refer to what is essentially the same 'condition'. Michael Brown, in *Psychodiagnosis in Brief*,[35] makes personality disorder and character disorder synonymous, and includes several conditions others will regard as distinctively different from character disorder as described here. Paul Ware[14] uses 'antisocial personality' to refer to a 'personality adaptation' and then defines five other adaptations (hysterical, schizoid, passive-aggressive, paranoid, and obsessive compulsive), none of which necessarily constitutes a pathological 'disorder' in itself, but only when it becomes extreme or persistent. As Michael Brown points out, 'most people experience or act in some of these ways some of the time.'[35] *ICD 9* (the World Health Organization's *International Classification of Diseases*, 9th Revision)[29] includes under 'Personality Disorders', in Category 301, a variety of 'deeply ingrained maladaptive patterns of behaviour' including, at Classification 301.7, 'Personality Disorder with predominantly sociopathic or asocial manifestation' and in which there is 'gross disparity between behaviour and prevailing social norms'. Unfortunately, this leaves open the question of what constitutes 'gross' disparity. Until quite recently this would have included, for example, an unmarried girl becoming pregnant, any kind of homosexual encounter, or any heterosexual domestic partnership between unmarried couples. But the social and moral scene has changed.

Most of the published work on character disorder refers to severely damaged personalities, especially criminals. These are often referred by courts to probation officers and other statutory services but were, until recently, rarely seen in private practice. Such people can cause an enormous amount of distress to those who care about them and to the society they live in. I find that at any one time as many as half my private clients, though not identifiable as 'offenders', present character-disorder features, often without clear evidence of neurosis. Typically, the person experiences no serious distress within himself, as a neurotic would; his distress, and his need for counselling, is occasioned by someone else's reaction to his unacceptable behaviour.

Frederick S. Perls, the originator of Gestalt Therapy, confuses the issue by declaring 'Once you have a character you have developed a rigid system. Your behaviour becomes petrified, predictable, and you lose your ability to cope freely with the world with all your resources'.[36] So, from Perls's point of view, character itself seems to be a disorder! Clearly, there is a great deal of confusion, first about the diagnosis, and second about how to refer to it.

The term 'character disorder' can, I believe, be properly applied, without being pejorative or judgemental, to a wide range of non-criminal subjects whose behaviour deviates in some significant respect from the norm for the society in which they live. 'Norm' is used here in the sociological sense of 'an established standard of behaviour shared by members of a social group to which each member is expected to conform'.[7] The deviation does not need to be of criminal proportions before it leads to relationship problems and emotional distress. The primary difficulty is in establishing what *is* the social norm. Perls has said, 'The whole idea of good or bad, right and wrong, is always a matter of boundary, of which side of the fence I'm on'. But he also pointed out, 'I'm talking about the human organism *per se* ... not about ourselves as social beings'.[36]

But, of course, we *are* social beings, and the diagnosis of character disorder has meaning only in a social context. We can be neurotic or psychotic in total isolation and suffer in our own minds. But the character-disordered person might not 'suffer' in his own mind at all. He is likely to do whatever he wants to do in a relatively uninhibited way until others react against him. At that point he might feel rejected, confused, and depressed, and perhaps will seek counselling on his own initiative.

Diagnostic Criteria

Character disorder is a difficult condition to diagnose precisely unless the person is so severely damaged as to be a persistent and convicted criminal. Some relatively 'normal' people might be regarded as criminal after committing a single offence which was 'out of character', while many character-disordered persons might never be convicted of a criminal offence at all. This might be because their deviance did not actually constitute a crime or, perhaps, because they managed to avoid being caught. The following criteria, however, are helpful to the professional counsellor in knowing what features to look out for.

The character-disordered person has relatively little real understanding of moral values and will probably have no conscience about personal behaviours that are commonly recognized as 'wrong'. They will often lie when there is really no need to, possibly because lying is just more exciting than telling the truth. He or she is frequently of good intelligence, possibly above average, which enables them to get around laws and to rationalize immoral behaviour. Anxiety is rarely a serious problem for them and they are unlikely to develop conditions such as ulcers, colitis, asthma, diabetes, eczema, and other diseases generally believed to have a strong emotional component. They might even be regarded as particularly well adjusted because they are unlikely to embarrass others with displays of neurotic emotion! They present themselves well with a 'good front', often being well dressed and with an attractive personality, even subservient or ingratiating if it suits them, so that they are good con-men – or con-women. Character disorder has no gender boundaries but is almost certainly more common in men (as is neurosis in women) because women usually have the primary responsibility for parenting and so tend to develop a stronger Parent ego state.

Because they do not get close to people and tend to be emotionally shallow and to lead rather impersonal sex lives, CDs are rarely able to form enduring personal relationships, especially with the opposite sex. They don't plan ahead, don't set realistic goals, and therefore set themselves up to lose, at least in the final analysis – the more serious cases probably finishing up in prison. Perhaps the most outstanding feature of the character-disordered person is his disinclination to accept responsibility. Whatever goes wrong, he sees it as someone else's fault, or perhaps just bad luck. Commonly, his Life Position (*see* Chapter 7) is I'm OK – You're Not OK; he commonly has a paranoid personality adaptation in addition to being antisocial, and so control is likely to be a big issue for him. No one is going to push him around! He therefore rejects authority. He lives essentially for himself and, despite his relatively high intelligence, he makes the same mistakes time after time.

We do not, of course, need to identify *all* of these features to make a diagnosis of character disorder. Appendix C provides a questionnaire that can be used by practitioners for determining to what extent, if any, a client might be character disordered. It can also be useful if the client is asked to complete this independently as a self-diagnosis.

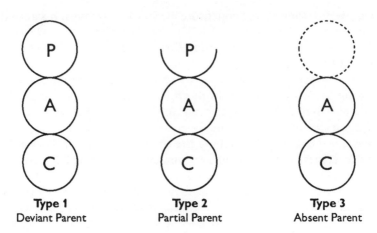

Figure 10 Three Types of Character Disorder

Shea Schiff has provided a useful contribution to the TA under-standing of character disorder, describing three distinct types, diagrammed in Figure 10 above. The structural diagram for Type 1 looks exactly like that of a 'normal' person. He is perceived as having a fully integrated Parent ego state with a coherent system of beliefs and values – but they are different from those prevailing in society at large. These values might be shared and reinforced by his parents and other members of his own family. Examples of this might include a member of the Mafia or a sincere revolutionary, perhaps a terrorist, for whom killing innocent people, including children, is classified as praiseworthy behaviour pursued in the interests of some overriding political ideal. Other members of a terrorist 'organization' might be committed to various forms of crime, such as armed robbery, drug trafficking, and arms dealing, which are all seen as part of the 'armed struggle'. Outside the political arena (which, for the terrorist at any rate, is his controlling belief system) he might have very rigid social values – for example, about the integrity of marriage.

Type 2 has a partial Parent ego state. He might have apparently clear beliefs and values in some areas of life but he will tend to sit loose to them. He lacks a coherent moral system which will guide him along life's path without coming into avoidable conflict with other people, society in general, or the law. This is the type most commonly seen in private practice. A typical example is 'Richard', who maintains apparently firm beliefs in relation to such issues as personal integrity, environmental pollution, animal rights, and freedom of the press but is sexually promiscuous and applies his own belief system when it comes to the law regarding the use of drugs. His close relationships tend to be brief and stressful, leading to depression. Another example is 'Conrad' who lives comfortably, runs a car, and enjoys holidays abroad on fraudulently obtained State Benefits when he is quite capable of earning a living in full-time, productive work. But he prefers voluntary work, including counselling for the Drug and Alcohol Council.

Type 3 character disorders seem to have no Parent ego state at all, although they can 'act parental' from a refined Adult ego state. This can be confusing because they sometimes appear to have good social values, perhaps holding office in local or national government. This is, of course, an Adult 'cover' for their true character, and is part of their elaborate system for 'conning' people. It would be easy – but perhaps legally dangerous – to suggest well-known contemporary examples of Type 3 character disorder. It is not humanly possible to know *everything* about any person and to understand the motivation, or even justification, for certain antisocial, even criminal, behaviours. Any appraisal, therefore, is likely to be seen as judgemental in some counselling circles and even libellous to the subject or his family! Furthermore, Type 3 character disorders are not necessarily more antisocial than Types 1 and 2. In fact, their well-developed intelligence often enables them to anticipate, and so avoid, at least for the time being, the social rejection others might incur.

A feature of character disorder often overlooked by politicians, therapists, and law professionals is the excitement factor. Typical of this is an offender sentenced to Community Service who was asked by his Supervisor what he did for a living. 'I'm a chef', he answered. 'Worked on the *QEII*. Cook you anything – bangers and chips or baked armadillo in clay.' The Supervisor asked, 'With talents like that, why commit crime?' He answered with a grin, 'The thrill of it all'. More obviously, some of the commonest crimes are vandalism and 'twocking' – taking vehicles without the owner's consent – all entirely non-profit-making.

Diagnostic criteria and references tend to come from the world of crime because that is where character disorder manifests most readily; the person is diagnosed by 'the system' and is sometimes sent for treatment. But many other people in our society are character disordered in accordance with the criteria I have described, and some of them might be impressively successful, even charismatic. Most commonly their relationships break down repeatedly, they are likely to react with depression and might then look for a counsellor on their own initiative. Others will seek counselling as an Adult (or Little Professor) way of dealing with a partner who threatens to leave them if they don't! Some form homosexual or lesbian relationships that might bring them into conflict either with others in society (perhaps their families) or with their own prejudicial Parent programming, leading to distress and the need for a counsellor. Yet others seek comfort, hope, or excitement in a variety of pornographic, occult, violent, or abusive behaviours, for example; if these come for counselling it is likely to be on someone else's initiative. Some, who are sincerely seeking for some meaning in life but get lost on the journey, decide to become counsellors or therapists themselves. They then might find the treatment they need (and perhaps want) in the context of training.

From a clinical point of view, the issue is not whether the behaviours associated with character disorder are 'right' or 'wrong' but whether they are functional in terms of the person's ability to enjoy peace of mind, a sense of personal well-being, and the ability to form mutually rewarding, long-term relationships.

12 Responding to Character Disorder

The Rehabilitation of the Parent Ego State

The characteristics of the Parent ego states have already been detailed in Chapter 2. These considerations bear so strongly on the use of transactional analysis in contemporary counselling, however, that I need make no apology if some of the material in Chapter 2 is repeated and reinforced here. From the earliest days of TA, the Parent ego state has tended to get a bad press because it prevented people from freely doing their own thing. It suppressed spontaneous emotion and natural urges, particularly sexual, thus promoting frustration, resentment, anxiety, guilt, and neurotic manifestations. But all too often the negative influence of P1, responding to non-verbal messages from the Child ego state of the parents, has been confused with P2, the essential characteristics of which, as Steiner[4] has perceived, are normally benign and constructive. Although the term 'Controlling Parent' is now generally used, early TA writers (Dusay[54], James[42] and others) used 'Critical Parent' and, while the adjective has changed, the attitude dies hard. Parents are, in fact, still thought of as being 'critical' – perhaps more so than ever before. When parents are less critical than those of earlier generations it might be that they themselves are unsure about what boundaries to prescribe, not only for their children but also for themselves.

There is still a tendency to regard criticism as essentially destructive when every responsible parent knows that the withholding of criticism from a youngster who misbehaves is likely to be interpreted as permission to do as he pleases, no matter how antisocial or self-destructive that might be. So responsible criticism *for the youngster's sake* is often a necessary element in the process of good parental nurturing.

Steiner[4] reserved the term 'Critical Parent' for P1, introducing the term 'Pig Parent' to emphasize its toxic influence. Now that we speak of Parent ego state functions as Caring and Controlling, it is easier for us to recognize the Parent as a power for good – always provided that the parents themselves have been well parented. Increasingly, however, this is not the case.

As already noted in Chapter 2, the essential quality of good parenting was enshrined in law in the 1969 *Children & Young Persons Act*. Section 1, Sub-Section 2(d) stated that a child might be made subject to a Supervision Order or even placed in the care of the Local Authority 'if the Court is of the opinion that ... he is in need of care or control which he is unlikely to receive unless the court makes such an order'. 'Care', the Act says, 'includes protection and guidance; and control includes discipline.'[8] The 'care and control' element is retained in subsequent legislation.

The liberation which began in the 1960s no doubt enabled many children, who might otherwise have been oppressed and psychologically abused, to grow up and achieve something of their real potential. But, at the same time, it has contributed to a generation, many of whose Parent ego states are minimal, with no general consensus about what the contents 'ought' to be. In addressing character disorder, therefore, there must be a particular emphasis on the strengthening, and perhaps re-programming, of the Parent ego state. This will not be *instead* of dealing with Script elements centred on P1, but additionally. In view of the variety of opinions about the desired 'content' of P2, however, this is likely to be an area of controversy.

Berne's concept of *Physis*, dealt with briefly in Chapter 8, is particularly relevant to this discussion and also merits some reinforcement. Berne says:

> The growth force, or Physis, which we see evidence of in the individual and society, works along with the superego, so that the individual has an urge to grow and to behave 'better' ... Both superego and Physis, if normal, oppose crude or brutal expressions of Id wishes. They start the individual off in not soiling his nappies and end up in the ideals of the United Nations.[22]

These extracts are from *A Layman's Guide to Psychiatry and Psychoanalysis*, which Berne wrote before he had developed transactional analysis, and before the Parent ego state had been named. For our purposes, however, it is unnecessary to make a distinction between Freud's superego and Berne's Parent ego state. Freud says of the origins of the superego:

> The parents' influence naturally includes not merely the personalities of the parents themselves but also the racial, national, and family traditions handed on through them as well as the demands of the immediate social *milieu* which they represent. In the same way, an individual's superego in the course of his development takes over contributions from later successors and substitutes of

his parents, such as teachers, admired figures in public life or high social ideals ... essentially the influence of what is taken over from other people.[28]

The same is true of the Parent ego state. Berne regarded *Physis* – 'the growth force of nature' – as a force that depends upon parental nourishment if it is to ensure the individual's growth and his capacity to 'take the happiness of others into consideration'[22] – that is, if he is to become functional as a member of society. That nourishment requires both care and control.

Therapeutic Considerations

There is a wide variety of techniques and therapeutic options that can be used successfully in private practice and in, say, a probation or even a prison setting with CD clients who are not habitual criminals. Experienced practitioners will already be familiar with these and some are included in Chapter 13 of this book. There are, however, several guiding principles which I find it is important to have in mind when working with even non-criminal CDs.

1 Treatment or management?

An important preliminary consideration is whether 'treatment' of character disorder is a realistic option at all. My long experience as a probation officer clearly demonstrated that many severely damaged subjects with a character disorder are unlikely to respond to a therapeutic programme aimed at fundamental change. The nature of the condition is such that they are rarely well motivated, and all too often they have a highly developed Adult ego state that is sharply in touch with the realities of here and now, and their experience convinces them that they are clever enough to handle a situation by *appearing* to change without actually changing!

Those diagnosed as 'character neurotics', however, often *can* be treated and so, I believe, can some who present no evidence of serious neurosis but have at least a 'partial' Parent ego state, as described by Schiff and diagrammed in Figure 10 in Chapter 11. Subjects with a deeply entrenched criminal disposition are probably treatable only on a relatively long-term basis in a therapeutic community or 'total learning environment' in a secure residential setting dedicated to that purpose, such as the psychiatric prison at Grendon, near Aylesbury. Mashud Hoghugi, working at the Aycliffe Children's

Centre, had some success using behavioural techniques with disturbed and often delinquent youngsters who were probably pre-character disordered; but this approach, as with the Schiff treatment programme for young schizophrenics, also presented political problems. Hoghugi's work, however, is well documented in his books *Assessing Problem Children*[37] and *Treating Problem Children*.[38] Probation officers and other professionals working with persistent offenders on an 'out-patient' basis or even in institutions which do not provide a total learning environment, can use TA principles for the better *management* of their clients but cannot be too optimistic about the outcome of 'treatment' if some fundamental change of character is looked for.

2 The therapeutic stance

Schiff has recommended that the practitioner working with a character disorder should eliminate from his 'stance' five elements that might otherwise be taken for granted as professionally appropriate, perhaps essential. He has said that the practitioner should: eliminate predictability, hope, fairness, trust, and the expectation that people should help![39] Each requires some comment:

1 *Eliminate predictability.* CDs love to 'make fools of people', especially those in positions of authority. The client himself is likely to be unpredictable. He may or may not keep his appointments, arrive on time, pay his fees and may or may not fulfil homework assignments and other contracts. But he will probably do enough of these things to encourage the counsellor to believe that it is worth while carrying on. Being 'in treatment' can have advantages, especially if one has to go to court or if indulgence or 'understanding' is called for from a disillusioned spouse or employer.

If the therapist is entirely predictable the CD client is likely to take mischievous advantage of the fact. He enjoys, above all, a bit of excitement and drama, so if the therapist wants to avoid being made a fool of he would do well to initiate the excitement himself by changing times, venues and therapeutic approaches, etc.

2 *Eliminate hope.* Hope, says Schiff, is what people do instead of solving problems. CDs will often 'try hard' if they have received this counter-injunction from a parent or parent substitute. But rarely will they have the characteristic of 'endurance' Clarkson refers to, which lifts it from the Driver mode into an Allower or Permission.[31] Rather than take constructive initiatives to change his circumstances, the

CD tends to hope that 'things', or other people, will change, that he'll come up on the pools, meet a more attractive partner or that the one she or he already has will change into a prince or princess. The counsellor will not, of course, buy into this fantasy, but the client has to learn, perhaps painfully, that he himself must change in some significant respect if his life is to be enriched.

3 *Eliminate fairness.* Fairness, say Schiff, is a Loser's concept. The reality is that we live in an unfair world and if the CD is going to wait for it to become 'fair' he will wait for ever. Also, 'fairness' is a concept that has its origins in the Parent ego state. It is how we believe things 'ought' to be. If the concept of fairness were firmly programmed into his own Parent ego state, it is unlikely that he would need counselling in the first place. So eliminate fairness; the *severely* character-disordered client probably has no idea what it means.

(This principle, I believe, holds good for the *management* of habitual criminals and other seriously damaged CDs. But in *treatment* of non-criminal character-disordered clients, which is aimed at change and personal growth – and is probably the goal in private practice – the client must learn the value of 'fairness' and obviously must see it modelled, where appropriate, by the therapist.)

4 *Eliminate trust.* The issue is that CDs in general are not trustworthy – and no one but a fool will trust an untrustworthy person. One of the CD's basic problems is that he has never learned to trust other people, parents in particular, and he will never become trustworthy until he has learned from experience that people *can* be trusted. He must learn what trust is like and he must learn it from the counsellor. So the counsellor must be worthy of the client's trust even when the client is not worthy of the counsellor's.

5 *Eliminate the expectation that people should help.* Most practitioners will be quite comfortable with this stance because it is a basic expectation of counselling that the client is encouraged to help himself. But it should be emphasized that this elimination is more than just an injunction against 'Rescuing', which usually involves helping people who have not asked for help in an Adult way. Some CDs will ask for help when they are quite capable of managing without it, on the basis of 'What's the good of having a dog and barking yourself!'

These Five Eliminations are useful guidelines to have 'at the back of one's mind' in dealing with all cases of character disorder. Schiff clearly developed them for working with more difficult subjects, however, so they need to be used with sensitivity and discrimination.

Most character-disordered clients are not habitual criminals, even though most criminals are character disordered!

3 Contracting

It is just as important to make clear contracts, as discussed in Chapter 10, with CDs as with any other client but frequently, I find, it is more difficult. They rarely want to change anything in themselves except, perhaps, to *feel* better while continuing to behave in the same way! Frequently, they really want someone else to change. So it is important to have a clear remit and, to begin with, this should be around the counselling situation itself rather than the client's long-term goals, because many CDs do not readily see ahead, except, perhaps, in unrealistic fantasy. A series of 'mini-contracts' is usually the best in the early stages – for example, to obtain information about flats or houses and bring it to the next session, rather than to decide too soon to be in his own home within three months. It is important that the client learns the significance of commitment, of making realistic working agreements, completing homework assignments and carrying them through. Similarly, the counsellor should stick by *his* agreements. For example, six sessions 'to test the water' should be six sessions precisely, followed by termination. It should be left entirely to the client's own initiative to telephone and make a further appointment after that.

4 A structured approach

TA is a particularly appropriate model to use in working with CDs because it lends itself to a structured approach. The CD will fill in a great deal of time to no great purpose if he is allowed to, perhaps hoping that the therapist will eventually 'do something' to put everything right. After a while he might decide he's spent enough on it and terminate, often without notice, even if he has undertaken to give the two clear sessions' notice of unilateral termination that I usually ask for. The CD reacts against authority, discipline, and structure but, having done so, he is lost without it! Secretly he is seeking for someone to provide the clear guidance, boundaries, and parenting that he never had as a child, which is why he so often ends up in the hands of the police or on probation or even in prison where some authority figure will take charge and provide the security he so desperately needs. The same need for structure and authority might also be met by certain religious sects or denominations.

After a new client has given an account of his situation and we have established some kind of working relationship, I usually ask him to read my own little book *Taking Charge of Your Own Life*[40] and to answer the questions on p. 11. If the client demonstrates some commitment and insight in this phase, it might be worth while proceeding; otherwise probably not. The counsellor should be familiar with the characteristics of the antisocial personality described in Chapter 11, if he is to avoid being caught up in a confusing, frustrating, and unfruitful therapeutic enterprise.

5 *Doors to therapy*

In his paper, 'Personality Adaptations (Doors to Therapy)', Paul Ware[14] suggests that the 'Contact Door' for CDs (for whom he uses the term Anti-Social) is Behaviour, with Feeling as the 'Target Door'. This model is also briefly referred to in Chapter 13. However severe the condition, the treatment approach is much the same. We begin by confronting the unacceptable behaviour, which is his 'Contact Door'. We then move to feelings, the 'Target Door' – perhaps by asking him what he *feels* about the way he is behaving and the distress he is causing. Some persistence might be necessary before the client's hard defensive shell is breached but eventually it can be, as a rule, because this client functions mainly from his Child ego state, and feelings, though heavily defended, are a primary behavioural determinant. Once he is in touch with his real feelings the client might then be in a position to think differently. But thinking is the 'Trap Door' so we are unlikely to make much progress addressing him initially on a purely cognitive level. He is clever and will outsmart the therapist!

6 *Using the Adult ego state*

The character-disordered client tends to be above average intelligence and often has a well-developed Adult ego state which he uses to work out how to care for and control himself in the absence of a coherent and more spontaneous internalized Parent ego state. The CD's Adult, however, is likely to be heavily contaminated with Child and early therapeutic work will be concerned with decontamination.

My own experience bears out Paul Ware's inclusion of 'Don't be a child' as an injunction typical of the antisocial personality or character disorder. Unfortunately, this does not necessarily issue in 'grown-up' behaviour. The person is more likely to behave in ways he mistakenly *perceives* as grown-up – such as getting drunk, having a multitude of sexual partners, or driving fast cars regardless of whether he is legally entitled to do so! Because the 'Target Door' is Feeling, however, it is tempting, in therapy, to encourage the client to 'get into Child', especially in a group situation. But this can sometimes be counterproductive with the CD until treatment is well advanced. He has not usually been oppressed with the heavy parenting typical of the neurotic and is unfamiliar with feelings of authentic guilt. Although he has usually received some toxic Script messages from the Parent-in-the-Child ego state (P1) of his Mother and Father, his own Child ego state is often relatively free and uninhibited. That is, in fact, the problem!

The CD needs his Adult ego state to serve as a substitute Parent ego state until such time as he can, if possible, develop the real thing. If he has at least a partial Parent to begin with, this might be realistic; if not he might have to rely on the Parent-in-the-Adult, or Ethical Parent. Berne, in *Transactional Analysis in Psychotherapy*, merely outlines the idea of an Ethical Adult 'integrated into the neopsychic ego state', and he acknowledges that 'the mechanism of the "integration" remains to be elucidated' and is 'the most obscure area in structural analysis, so that it is not possible at present to clarify it clinically'. But the task of clarifying it clinically might be one of the most urgent tasks for counsellors and psychotherapists to address in the present moral and social climate. Significantly, Berne observes that 'Such advanced structural analysis may be desirable in working with character problems'.[3]

The concept of the integrated Adult, touched upon in Chapter 2, is one of Berne's several undeveloped ideas. It has profound spiritual implications which, along with the concept of *Physis*, might point the way forward for all who have enough insight to recognize their own need, not least those with character disorder. This is explored further in the final chapter of this book and is also referred to in Appendix A, for advanced practitioners.

7 *Watch for the Demon*

All ego states can manifest in either a constructive or destructive way, and the CD's Natural Child is frequently anything but constructive! Another of Berne's undeveloped contributions to our understanding of human behaviour is his concept of the Demon, to which he devotes four paragraphs in *What Do You Say After You Say Hello?*[5] The Demon appears to be the Negative Free Child, is so featured on the New Ego State Model, and is detailed in Chapter 2. It is the

Natural Child ego state that has not been subjected to the whole-some, nurturing care and control normally provided by responsible parents. In consequence, it is free to be mischievous and destructive in a way that is more or less uninhibited.

The Demon should not be confused with the Rebellious Adapted Child that might be reacting in a creative and positive way to some kind of oppressive parenting.

It is essential for the CD to mobilize enough uncontaminated Adult for him to recognize that he has, in fact, 'scrambled his life', as Berne put it, and that the resultant mess is due not so much to Child ego state adaptations (either positive or negative) as to no adapt-ations at all! When parents are themselves unclear about where behavioural boundaries lie they cannot provide either the guidance required for effective 'care' or the discipline required for 'control'. They then feed the power of the Demon and, unless there is some effective therapeutic intervention, can promote its growth into adolescence and adulthood. This commonly results in rebellion and defiance, not against his parents (with whom the Demon might be in league anyway) but against the demands and conventions of society at large which, as soon as he gets to school, tries to restrict his freedom. In a word, he is unsocialized.

8 Caring confrontation

Many clients, and particularly young ones, I find, are so lacking in clear moral guidelines that they are like ships without rudders. Such clients are suffering, directly or indirectly, because they are 'anti-social' in some significant respect and are not conforming to the social norm. Just how we define what *is* the social norm, without being either prejudiced or judgemental, is a problem each therapist must resolve for herself in the light of her own 'norms' as a profes-sional carer. But it is imperative that client and therapist reach broad areas of agreement about where the behavioural boundaries lie. In the absence of such agreement there is nothing that can legitimately be confronted as a behavioural deviation. But having agreed the boundaries, then caring Confrontation must be the keynote.

It is beyond the counsellor's remit to *impose* his own belief system on a client, even if the belief system is transactional analysis! But the notion that everyone should 'think his beliefs out for himself' is, in my view, absurd, unless the person has some foundations on which to build. The goal may, indeed, be an 'integrated Adult' incorpo-rating those Parent introjects that have been checked out by the Adult ego state. But frequently, the only Parent introjects available have been based on 'what everybody does' – which is not, of course, 'everybody' at all but usually an influential peer group well publicized in the media. Nevertheless, any deviation from that position might be quite 'unthinkable', especially for a character-disordered person programmed with a 'Don't think' injunction. So it might be the counsellor's responsibility to question the client's assumptions and to help him check out in Adult what assumptions or beliefs are functional.

This is, I believe, the central core of the problem of treating and of managing clients who are character disordered. It is a nettle that is particularly uncomfortable for those of us to grasp who have, and perhaps even welcome, a character-disorder element in our own personality structure, rather than an over-responsible 'neurotic' tendency, which is frequently the perceived alternative.

13 Practical Counselling

Neurosis, said C.G. Jung, is a substitute for legitimate suffering. So therapy begins with suffering. Unless a person is suffering in some way – psychologically, emotionally, or because of a stressful relationship – they will have no need of a therapist or counsellor. If they are to stop suffering, they must change permanently in some significant way that will affect their entire *modus operandi*. Many people seek therapy because they *feel* bad about themselves in some way; they feel inferior or inadequate or depressed or anxious or phobic, for example, and all they ask for is that they will in the end feel 'happy'. But real change will involve all three dimensions of human experience – feeling, thinking, and behaviour – and to accomplish this can demand a considerable effort of will and a lot of commitment.

Allen Wheelis, in *How People Change*,[41] defines the sequence of therapy as Suffering, Insight, Will, Action, Change. The suffering brings the person to the therapist and the process of therapy promotes insight. With the insight, the person wills or desires to change and ratifies that decision by doing something different – by going into action. But the new action, the new style of behaviour, thinking and feeling, must be practised continually before significant and enduring change takes place. In a graphic illustration, Wheelis describes how an honest man might set about becoming a thief! Obviously, he must steal, not just once but repeatedly, devoting his life to stealing until it becomes 'second nature', and eventually he does it without thinking. And so with any other significant change. It must be practised repeatedly and continually until it becomes normal. Finally, with commitment to the process of change, the person can find what he is looking for – a new direction in life.

Because this book is an 'explorer's handbook' and not a treatment manual, I include this chapter with some degree of caution. I believe, however, it is appropriate to offer readers some insight into how a Transactional Analysis Psychotherapist might actually work in responding to client needs. Most text-books are written by authorized teachers of TA and must, therefore, teach an officially recognized and approved style of therapy. The present writer, however, is a 'Certified

Transactional Analyst Specialising in Clinical Applications' (CTA) but not a Teaching and Supervising Transactional Analyst (TSTA). Like any practitioner, I have developed my own unique style and approach and, while this does not deviate greatly from what is approved by the TA establishment, it does not purport to be 'authoritative' as an introduction to the practice of transactional analysis. With that caveat, therefore, I offer this outline sketch of the kind of things I do when working with clients. Also included, for the reader's interest, is a sketch of the Cathexis approach to working with young schizophrenics which I do *not* use because the method is designed for use in a residential setting. The examples that follow should not, of course, be used in therapy except by practitioners who have some training, experience and expertise, though not necessarily in transactional analysis. Responsible professionals will, in any event, be exploring further in the books referred to where a more detailed account of therapeutic techniques and procedures can be found. The ideas are not presented in any particular order, though I normally deal with the question of confidentiality at the outset so that I and my new client both know where we stand.

The Counselling Relationship

I first trained in the 1960s as a probation officer for whom 'casework' was the appropriate professional skill. Casework is social work based on a close study of the personal histories and circumstances of individuals and families. This, of course, involved an element of counselling but I quickly found that the Freudian psychoanalytic philosophy which underpinned casework in those days was unhelpful when it came to engaging, face to face, with my clients. Fortunately, I soon discovered transactional analysis, which was just beginning to be taught and practised in Britain, and my work then took on a whole new dimension, which meant that, not only did I know what I was doing, but my clients could know as well. One of the books to which I was introduced in the course of my training was *The Casework Relationship* by Felix P. Boesteck, which recommended eight 'principles' of good casework. They are all important but the one I found most challenging was 'Controlled Emotional Involvement'. Psychoanalysts and others, basing their work on that theory, are usually skilled at avoiding emotional involvement with their clients for that would cloud their detached scientific judgement. But I have never found it easy. I have no difficulty with the emotional involvement but I sometimes do with the control!

I mention this rather personal experience at this stage because I believe I am not alone among counsellors and therapists in having difficulty in this area of my work. Counsellors are rarely detached scientists. We care deeply about people and especially about our clients. Some emotional involvement with them is necessary and desirable but control is imperative, or we begin to have a personal investment in the outcome of our counselling work. This is one of the most important areas for professional supervision which is dealt with at the end of this chapter.

Confidentiality

Most clients coming to see a counsellor, even for the first time, are likely to assume that whatever transpires within the therapeutic relationship is entirely confidential. This means that nothing of a confidential nature will be divulged to anyone else. The client is then free to talk with the therapist about sensitive material he or she might never have previously disclosed to anyone, and is sure that this confidence will be respected.

While this is essentially true there are, or should be, boundaries to confidentiality, and the client should be made aware of this as soon as possible. Having been trained as a probation officer, I quickly learned that to offer absolute confidentiality to clients, who were frequently character disordered and expert manipulators, was dangerous indeed! To have a man 'confess' that he had committed a murder or a robbery or that he had had sex with his own twelve-year-old daughter and then to be professionally obliged to leave him at large to do it again, is a situation best avoided! I made a practice, as a probation officer, of assuring my clients that I would treat all they told me as confidential but that they should trust me to use the information responsibly and in their best long-term interests. I also let them know that I, too, was under supervision and would, if necessary, share confidences with my professional supervisor. This left me free to consult others as necessary, on the client's behalf, and left the client free to share with me, if he wished, burdens that were troubling him.

I have adopted essentially the same policy in my counselling and psychotherapy practice. I assure my clients that whatever passes between us I will treat as confidential but that there are certain boundaries. In the first place I advise them that, like all professionally accredited practitioners, I consult regularly with a qualified colleague with whom I share some of the many burdens every practitioner must carry. (This is discussed at the end of this chapter.) Because I often tape-record therapy sessions, I also tell the client that I might play back parts of the recording to my supervisor-colleague so that we can discuss together what was going on in therapy. This is, of course, for the client's benefit and rarely have I had anyone object. The tape-recorder can always be switched off if necessary at the client's request.

In addition, I advise every client that, if at any time during therapy I feel, in my professional judgement, that the client might present a danger either to herself or to someone else, then I have a professional responsibility to do something about it. If I suspect the client is in danger of committing suicide, then I will usually advise her family doctor (whose details I request in completing an Intake Sheet) and perhaps try to arrange for admission to hospital. If I suspect the client is in serious danger of harming someone else, then I will consider it my responsibility to inform the police or the threatened person, or both. I know perfectly well, and frequently tell the client, that it is most unlikely that either the family doctor or the police will take any action until and unless the deed has been done. But defining these boundaries at the outset is, I find, helpful for the client as well as for me.

Intake

Certain basic information about a client's name, address, and telephone number is obviously necessary, and every practitioner will devise her own way of recording this. I include Date of Birth in case of later referral to a doctor who might need this for identification. I ask who the GP is, any consultant the client is seeing – especially, but not exclusively, psychiatrists or clinical psychologists. If the client is already in therapy with another practitioner for the condition they have come with, there might be an ethical problem that needs to be resolved as soon as possible. I ask what medication the client is taking and find out, later if necessary, what effects it is likely to have. I also ask what previous experience of counselling or other forms of therapy the client has had. After the client has gone, I make brief notes under such headings as: 'The Problem as Presented'; 'Current Stress' (unemployment, domestic friction, physical illness, etc.); 'Support System' (who, if anyone, has the client got to turn to when the going gets rough?); and briefly note our Initial Contract, if we have arrived at one, regarding fees, number of sessions, termination arrangements, goals, etc.

Diagnosis

For the transactional analyst, most diagnosis is about ego states, transactions, games, and scripts. In addition, we also take account of the client's stroking patterns and the way she structures her time, her rackety behaviour, and the modes of passivity she favours. We avoid where possible attaching 'labels' to the client, such as 'depressed' or 'agoraphobic', because this seems a dehumanizing way of treating our fellow beings. We don't ask what the client *is* – because we start from the premise that she is 'OK', as we ourselves are, even though it might not always seem like that! We ask instead what she *does* in terms of thinking, feeling, and behaviour. This is her own responsibility and she can change it when she has a mind to.

This principle might seem inconsistent with the last two chapters that focus on the distinction between neurosis and character disorder, either of which classification might seem 'dehumanizing'. But I am, whatever else, a pragmatist. I have a clear responsibility to help my clients solve problems. If I avoid giving a name – a 'label', if you like! – to the condition, whatever it is, that lies at the root of the trouble, I cannot communicate about it, even with myself reflectively, let alone with the client!

It is, of course, sometimes helpful to use diagnostic labels such as 'depression' or 'anxiety state' when communicating with other professionals, doctors in particular, and, in that event, it is wise to use the *International Classification of Diseases* which provides a system of nomenclature agreed by the World Health Organization.[29] Transactional analysts are often taught to use *DSM IV*, the *Diagnostic and Statistical Manual* of the American Psychiatric Association.[30] This is particularly detailed and comprehensive, providing for a clear treatment plan, and is a valuable aid to the therapist or counsellor. While psychiatrists will no doubt be familiar with it, however, other British doctors are less likely to be.

Group Treatment

Transactional analysis was originated by Berne as a method of group treatment. This was not for merely economic reasons but because he firmly believed that the group process was, in general, a much more potent means of facilitating change than individual treatment. Berne recognized that personal growth, whether you call it spiritual or psychological (and I would have difficulty in defining the difference), occurs in the context of relationship or else it does not occur at all! Whatever techniques we use in counselling and psychotherapy, few practitioners will question that it is the relationship between the client and the therapist that is the most potent instrument of change and growth. And, while 'love' is a word we must use with caution (because it is much abused and means different things to different people), it is love that, in the final analysis, promotes life and growth, and it is the absence of real, self-giving love that accounts for the multitude of ills that bring clients and counsellors together in search of it. So the therapy group is a kind of organism in which creative love is the life-giving spirit and in which Intimacy as a Time Structure is encouraged. In individual therapy and counselling there is a group of only two – but the same organic principle applies.

Much of what happens in modern TA therapy groups – and certainly in groups I have led – is, in fact, better described as individual treatment in a group setting rather than as group treatment as Berne himself practised it. Each client's interaction with other group members is still important, however, and gives opportunities for the therapist to help participants recognize that their behaviour towards one another in the group often reflects the pathology that brought them into treatment and might be a re-enactment of unresolved childhood issues. Also, clients in groups are, as a rule, enormously supportive of one another, and their relationships with one another might be at least as therapeutic as their relationship with the therapist.

Trainee transactional analysts will experience a good deal of group treatment in the client role, and will also take the therapist role from time to time to practise their skills. A particularly valuable experience is the 'marathon', a therapy group that extends over two or three days, sometimes more, giving each participant abundant opportunity to resolve developmental and Script issues which might otherwise take weeks or even months of less intensive work. At the beginning of each group session, whatever its length, the first task is to make 'session contracts'. Each participant declares what change he or she wishes to make during the course of the group session or marathon, which should be related to the overall therapeutic contract, and this is usually written up on the board for all to see. The whole group (not just the individual and the therapist) then has a commitment to facilitating the change each has proposed.

The techniques used in a therapy group are much the same as those used in individual therapy, the overall goal being to promote autonomy through spontaneity, intimacy, and awareness.

Counselling-room Equipment

Almost all transactional analysts work with a blackboard, or more likely a white wipe-off board. The principle that 'a picture is worth a thousand words' holds good when we are drawing any of the diagrams used in this book to help the client understand what is going on and how it affects him or her personally. Of course, all sorts of other things can usefully be written up as well, especially contract ideas, and it is a good idea to ask the client to do the drawing or writing himself to engage his active involvement.

Transactional analysts in training learn to record everything that happens on a cassette tape – with the client's permission, of course. This is partly so that they can 'play' segments of work to their teachers to get feed-back and later take carefully selected segments into the examination room when they go for their final 'board'. But the recording can also be enormously valuable when segments are played back during the session so that the client herself (and the counsellor!) can hear what has just taken place – which ego state was being used, for example. What did it sound like on reflection; and how did it feel to listen to it? It is possible to buy cassette recorders that have an electronic marker. When this is activated the tape can be rewound later to exactly the spot marked and be played back instantly.

If the counsellor can afford the equipment this technique can be considerably enhanced by the use of a video camera which will show the client his body language as well as playing back his voice. I have seen this demonstrated effectively in training workshops (particularly with Bob and Mary Goulding) but have never felt the need to invest in it for my own therapeutic work. Personally, I feel that such equipment is too obtrusive and, even if the client does get used to it and forget it is there, the relationship is likely to become too clinical and calculated so that what one gains on the roundabouts is lost on the swings.

I usually provide my clients with a small notebook in which I ask them to note, between sessions particularly, anything they want to remember to bring into the session later. Contracts and homework assignments are, of course, noted during the session but later they can note dreams or any matter of possible consequence they wish to bring for discussion.

Finally, a box of tissues should be available. The shedding of tears is the most fundamental of all human emotional reactions and usually starts at the moment of birth. Tears can express *any* emotion – anger, sadness, fear, or joy – and most people have learned to keep the feelings and the tears under strict control. The counselling room is the one place where it is altogether OK to weep, and the shedding of tears is often the breakthrough needed to get the work moving. A box of tissues to mop up with is an essential item of equipment.

Working with Ego States

The first thing we need to become aware of is which ego state we – and others – are using. Berne once said that, when a therapist is working with ego states, she is practising transactional analysis; if she is not working with ego states, she is *not* practising transactional analysis! Most of the troubles in the world are caused by people using an inappropriate ego state or using, perhaps, an Adult ego state that is contaminated by either Parent or Child influences. A major emphasis in TA therapy, therefore, is in helping the client to become aware of these contingencies so that she can correct them with a view to releasing her capacity for intimacy, spontaneity, and awareness. Given these three capacities, the person is said to be 'autonomous' – that is thinking, feeling, and behaving in response to her authentic 'self', her *Physis*, and not in response to negative parental or archaic messages and Early Decisions that underlie her Script.

So the client is helped to become aware of inappropriate behaviours and to this end he or she can expect to be confronted by the therapist or by other group members.

Analysing Transactions

Working out what's going on between people is what transactional analysis is all about. This process starts with what kind of transactions are going on between client and counsellor in the counselling room, and extends to what kind of transactions the client is having with other important people who are 'on stage' with them in their Script. These people might be important players they live with or work with or close friends; or they might be just neighbours and acquaintances they meet casually who are only 'bit players' with walk-on parts and not even a line to say. The theory of Transactions as outlined in Chapter 3 should be constantly in mind during counselling, and the client should be taught at an early stage what is involved.

Stroking and Time Structuring

All transactions involve a Stroke of some kind. The counsellor is Stroking the client in giving her his undivided attention; the client is Stroking the counsellor in seeking his help and, probably, in paying him. Because the giving and receiving of Strokes is fundamental to the whole business of staying alive, it is important for the client to learn how to do this, using the knowledge and understanding which the counsellor will share with her or him session by session, outlined in Chapter 4.

A proper understanding of Time Structuring is no less important because some ways of structuring time are more fruitful than others in terms of stroke uptake. Most clients are more or less stroke starved, because of the Stroke Economy on which most of us are brought up. So, whatever the client's problem, the more she learns about how to receive (and give) positive, life-enhancing Strokes the better. And frequently it is essential for the client to review what she is doing with her time, how much opportunity she is giving herself for collecting Positive Strokes by relating closely enough to other people for it to happen. For example, is she confined to her house and family? Is she attending any kind of class or group, a health club, or Weight Watchers? Is she a member of any organization such as the Women's Institute or Townswomen's Guild, or a church? Is she working and is the work rewarding or does she do voluntary work or just have coffee with the neighbours? Some people simply starve themselves of Strokes for scripty reasons that might need to be explored. A man gets few Strokes watching football on television at home; he would get many more by joining a football club or even by watching football on television at his local pub or club. Stroking and Time Structuring are important areas for exploration in counselling.

Analysing Games

One of the most important transactions for the client to become aware of is the Ulterior Transaction (*see* Figure 3) because this is so often the opening move in a psychological Game. Games can be diagrammed on the board by using either ego states or, better still, the Drama Triangle (Figure 4). If a 'name' can be assigned to the Game, such as NIGYSOB (Now, I've got you, son of a bitch) or Uproar or 'Why don't you ... Yes, but ...' the client is better able to remember it and to avoid it in future. It is also helpful sometimes to use Berne's Game Formula (Chapter 5) to help the client understand the sequence of events.

Exposing Rackets and Racket Feelings

Racket Feelings can occur spontaneously in fantasy with no one else involved at the time or they can arise as the pay-off at the end of a manipulative Game. In either event they are counterproductive to the client's well-being and need to be brought to light. A client who is, for example, wallowing in feelings of inferiority and lack of self-esteem, is almost certainly setting up these feelings in an on-going way. She is, as we say, 'running a Racket', the ulterior purpose of which is to manipulate other people into a Game with the promise of a Racket Feeling pay-off that will reinforce the client's Script. The counsellor must expose this behaviour.

Identifying Life Positions

It is quite possible that our temperaments, and hence our Basic Life Positions, are to some extent genetically determined. But there is little doubt that developmental factors also play an important role. To identify a client's Basic Life Position is an important element in Script analysis, and reference to the diagram in Figure 6 will show that a lot of valuable information can be inferred from it.

I often deal with Life Positions quite early in the work, particularly to identify which Escape Hatch the client might be most at risk of using. There is guidance on Escape Hatch closure later in this chapter.

Script Analysis

While Script Analysis is a feature of transactional analysis psychotherapy, counsellors will find it helpful to know something about what it involves and may wish to incorporate certain features of it in their work. The primary purpose is to discover what are the Script Messages the client has used as a basis for making his Early Decisions about the direction life is going to take. These Early Decisions, made intuitively and with limited understanding of what was really going on in his childhood world, were no doubt useful at the age of, say, three, in ensuring the youngster's emotional survival in a world of powerful giants; and having 'proved' them in childhood, the person is likely to continue to abide by these Early Decisions for the rest of his life when, in all probability, they are quite out of date and entirely inappropriate. Script analysis is concerned with discovering what these Early Decisions were and then taking therapeutic steps to change them and make new decisions which are more constructive for the present time.

The Developmental History and associated Background Information dealt with later in this chapter will help in the identification of Script Messages.

Confrontation

Someone has described confrontation as 'making public what is supposed to be kept secret'. 'The essential quality of good confrontation', say Woollams and Brown, 'is that it thwarts the client's attempt to establish a symbiosis, thereby inviting the client to do something different.'[16] Drawing the client's attention, by various means, to the counterproductive ways he or she is behaving in the therapy session is the primary means of achieving 'decontamination'.

Discounting, or 'not taking account' of various factors needful for problem solving, as described in Chapters 5 and 9, must be confronted continually and it is useful to have in mind *The Healthy Model*[10] quoted on p. 35.

A typical confrontation might go as follows:

THERAPIST: I see you are sitting pincer-toed with your finger in your mouth. Which ego state are you cathecting?
CLIENT: My Child, I suppose.
THERAPIST: Would a different ego state be more appropriate?
CLIENT: Adult?
THERAPIST: OK. So how will you go about cathecting Adult?
CLIENT: [*moves to a more relaxed position with legs crossed and hand under chin*].
THERAPIST: Is there anything else you have in mind?
CLIENT: Eye contact? Even voice?
THERAPIST: Fine. Now we're communicating.

Having made these behavioural changes the client actually feels differently and is free to think differently.

Or the therapist might comment, 'You said "I can't" in a very Adult tone of voice, as though that is a matter of fact. But is it? All I asked you to do was to reach out and take my hand. Your arm isn't paralysed, is it? How come you can't do a simple thing like that?'

CLIENT: I don't want to.
THERAPIST: OK. You can but you don't want to. Now you are being responsible.

The possibility that the client has had a bad experience in the past through being touched might be addressed straight away or later. This illustration of a decontaminating confrontation, however, serves also to indicate that actual physical contact between therapist and client is not nearly as 'taboo' in transactional analysis as it is in some therapies. But the practitioner needs to be well aware of what he or she is doing and why before using such a technique. It has obvious dangers.

A particular behaviour which the transactional analyst will confront is the Gallows Laugh. In brief, this means laughing, or perhaps just smiling, at something that is not funny. The expression is attributed to the apocryphal story of a highwayman who, as a naughty child, was told by his mother: 'You'll finish up on the gallows, you will!' When, twenty years later, he was caught and was awaiting execution, he laughed and said, 'My mother always said this would happen to me!' And the laugh somehow made his death easier to bear.

A client might say, with a laugh or a grin, 'I just hit him, like I always do'. Or, 'I was drunk, wasn't I? – Ha, ha'. The man doing Community Service, mentioned earlier, who was an expert chef and was asked why, with talents like that, he committed crime, said, with a mischievous twinkle in his eye, 'The thrill of it all'. He was laughing, implicitly, at something that was not funny!

The confrontation in any of those circumstances would probably be, 'Why did you laugh ... smile ... when you said that?'

The client might shrug and say, 'Well, you do, don't you! That's life!'

But the counsellor will not let it drop. He or she will probably say, 'What benefit is there in laughing at a behaviour that's caused you such unhappiness?'

The client might then reflect and acknowledge the foolishness of such laughter which, in fact, has the effect of reinforcing some self-destructive behaviour. If the counsellor actually laughs or smiles in return then a Gallows Transaction has taken place and, not only is the behaviour further reinforced, but the counsellor has also acknowledged that it is indeed funny and has effectively given the client permission to do it again!

Decontamination

Muriel James has said that contamination occurs 'when the clear thinking of the Adult is interfered with by the archaic feelings of the Child and/or the prejudicial feelings of the Parent'.[42] Parent contamination is probably seen by many as 'thinking' but we need to recognize that all thinking starts from assumptions about what is 'true', and these assumptions often have their roots in beliefs or prejudices invested in the Parent ego state. For example, an employer in Belfast who believes that Protestants are better than Catholics (or vice versa) is likely to start his reasoning with that assumption as a 'fact' when employing people for his work-force. Decontamination, therefore, means clearing away Child or Parent influences, either feelings or thoughts, that prevent the client from using his Adult ego state effectively.

Deconfusing the Child

This element in therapy is often associated with Decontamination, and either one might need to come first, depending on circumstances. At the risk of oversimplification 'deconfusing the Child' can mean enabling the client to become aware of, and perhaps express, her Child feelings and to distinguish between feelings, thoughts, and behaviours from C1 and Rackety or Adapted feelings, thoughts, and behaviours associated with P1 (see the New Ego State Model). Feelings associated with P1 will be *in response to* parental influences, those from C1 will be natural and spontaneous. But both kinds are 'authentic' in that they are entirely real to the client and both should be treated sensitively and with respect. There is an element of 'deconfusing the child' in the example above of decontamination, which involved touching the client.

Two-chair Work

One of the most commonly used techniques in TA therapy is 'two-chair work', in which the client sits first on one chair, then on another, to dialogue either between one ego state and another or, perhaps, between himself and a fantasy of mother or some other significant figure. Some therapists prefer to use cushions rather than chairs, especially if it is important for the client to 'get into Child'.

Two-chair work is particularly characteristic of Gestalt therapy. The object of the exercise is to bring the client's story into the here and now. For example:

THERAPIST:	Imagine your mother is sitting on this chair in front of you. Tell her what you are really feeling about her.
CLIENT [*to mother*]:	I love you because you're my mother. But I don't like you. You never seemed to love me. You always preferred Christopher.
THERAPIST:	Now go and sit on the other chair and *be* mother. Respond to what your daughter has just said to you.
CLIENT [*as Mother*]:	Of course I loved you. Christopher was younger so he had to have more attention.
CLIENT [*as self*]:	I always got left out. I always had to look after Christopher.
CLIENT [*as Mother*]:	I didn't intend to leave you out. I relied on you to help me ...

Through the dialogue the client is able to identify much more effectively with her mother as she was many years ago, bringing the past into the present. With the insight gained from this therapeutic experience she is now better able to decide that she will regard her mother differently in the light of mature understanding, which she did not have at the age of, say, four.

Letter Writing

I often ask a client to write a letter *as if* to his wife, mother, father, or some other important person, expressing thoughts and feelings he has been afraid to address directly to the person concerned. He will then bring the letter into therapy and read it to me. Doing this is, in itself, frequently quite cathartic. The letter usually provides abundant scope for exploring various aspects of the relationship in more detail.

It can then be helpful for the client to write another letter, for homework, which is the other person's *reply*. This kind of written work is, of course, similar to Two-chair Work and might be either a preparation for it or, perhaps, follow later if necessary. Sometimes, instead of writing a letter, the client comes to the next session having already found the resources to talk to the person directly.

The Redecision School

The Gouldings' Redecision School of transactional analysis, referred to in Chapter 8, draws particularly on Gestalt techniques. The Gouldings identified three 'impasses' within the personality where opposing forces meet in head-on collision and need to be resolved before the client is free to move ahead. The original Early Decision is made by the Little Professor – the Adult-in-the-Child – which is highly sensitive to the realities of here and now and whose primary role is to ensure the youngster's survival in a world of giants. Decisions made with such survival in mind at the age of five, however, are often counterproductive at the age of fifteen or fifty but might, nevertheless, still be in force if therapy, or some other experience, has not resulted in a change. For example, a person might have become aware that her way of thinking, feeling, and behaving is child-like in response to a 'Don't grow up' Injunction. But all her Adult efforts to be mature and autonomous are frustrated by an Early Script Decision saying 'I will always be a Child to please my Dad'. Her Creative Natural Child (C1) is in conflict with her Little

Professor (A1) which made a very smart Decision in the here-and-now of many years before. In Redecision Therapy the client will be asked to re-live in imagination a childhood scene in which the Early Decision was made or reinforced. Using two chairs or cushions C1 ('I want to grow up') will argue it out with A1, which made the Early Decision in the first place ('It's safer to stay little') until A1, with the benefit of the grown-up experience and understanding of *today's* here-and-now, wins the battle and makes a more appropriate New Decision or Redecision, such as: 'From now on I'm going to think, feel and behave as an adult, not as a child.'

Another person might have a strong 'Work hard' Counter-injunction message from his parents which is in conflict with a genuine Natural Child desire to slacken off and take things easy when middle life arrives and a heart attack is the likely outcome if he doesn't. The result is that until the impasse is resolved he can neither work hard effectively nor relax and look after his physical health.

The impasses or stuck points occur when the client is motivated to do one thing from one ego state and to do something else from another ego state. When the impasse is recognized and the therapeutic work is contracted for by the Adult (A2), the Little Professor (A1) is again the intuitive resource of wisdom which makes the New Decision just as, in childhood, it made the Early Decision for purposes of survival then.

The Gouldings say, 'We use behaviour modification, Gestalt, desensitization, psychodrama, anything that will facilitate the patient getting into his Child ego state in an archaic scene, making sure that he or she is there with affect, reliving the scene, and then making a new decision.'[18]

Notice of Termination

It is wise, when starting work with a client, to prepare her for the possibility that, when she is faced, during therapy, with painful or uncomfortable realities or memories of past experience, she might (in her Child ego state) want to discontinue the work. Some clients simply fail to turn up for an appointment, or telephone or write and cancel with some excuse. Others might suddenly find work in a distant town! Sometimes, termination might be the right thing for them to do; on other occasions it will be quite the wrong thing at that stage. The therapist will usually have a strong intuitive feeling which it is.

To safeguard against this situation, I ask my clients early in therapy to agree that they will not terminate unilaterally – that is, without my agreement – unless they give me two clear sessions' notice. This gives us the chance to deal with any issues that might go unresolved or be carried over into work with another therapist later on. Few decline to make this contract and certainly it has saved many clients from failing to complete what they have started.

Closing Escape Hatches

One of the most crucial new decisions for a client to make – and the earlier in therapy the better – is a decision to solve whatever problem has brought him to a therapist and not to cop out entirely from the responsibility for solving problems when the going gets rough. This calls for an Adult decision made in consultation with the therapist. This procedure, called 'Closing Escape Hatches', was referred to briefly in Chapter 7, which might be reread in association with this section.

What is called for is a decision that 'No matter what happens and no matter how bad things get, I will not kill myself or anyone else, either deliberately or by accident and I will not go crazy.'[18] I would emphasize that this requires an Adult *decision* by the client for his own sake, in the light of reality; it must not be seen as a promise to the therapist, which can easily be an ulterior Child–Parent transaction. Some therapists simply ask the client to make a 'no suicide contract' but I find it is better to deal with all three escape hatches together, usually early in therapy. It is surprising how many clients have harboured a secret desire to kill someone or a secret fear of going mad which might not surface if the matter is not addressed directly in this way.

Most people recognize that they do have a responsibility to solve problems rather than to try to escape that responsibility by killing themselves or someone else deliberately. But how can they avoid doing either of these things 'by accident'? Accidental 'suicide' can be achieved, for example, by overindulgence in alcohol, leading to either alcohol poisoning or, perhaps, an avoidable road accident in which the driver dies. The same carelessness might, of course, also lead to killing someone else but that would not be a breach of the contract unless the victim was someone we actually *wanted* to see dead. We might, however, kill someone else by accident, not intending to, if we hit the person in anger and he or she suffers or reacts in an unexpected way, perhaps by having a heart attack or striking his or her head on a sharp object when falling.

Some people have difficulty with deciding not to 'go crazy' because mental illness, and especially psychosis, is now generally supposed by medical science to be caused by biochemical imbalances over which the patient is deemed to have no control. The question of what caused the biochemical imbalance is rarely given much consideration, however, and drugs are used to relieve the symptoms anyway. But many psychiatrists recognize that, while there might well be a biochemical *predisposition* to mental illness, the trigger which actually precipitates it is often either intrapsychic or environmental stress or possibly a combination of both. The answer then to 'How can I decide not to go crazy?' lies in a decision to 'hang on to the joy-stick'. The image for this metaphor is of the pilot of a small plane who runs into a storm. His little aircraft is tossed about, as anyone might be tossed about by 'the storms of life'. If the pilot 'hangs on to the joy-stick', the control column of his aircraft, he will fly through the storm and come out safely at the other side. But if he panics and lets go of the joy-stick then he is likely to get into a flat spin and his aircraft – that is his life – will crash!

'Hanging on to the joy-stick' might be far from easy for a client under severe stress, and providing support in such a situation is an important responsibility for the therapist. If a client is unwilling to make an open-ended contract to close all Escape Hatches, he or she might agree to stay alive (or whatever) for, say, three months or even just until the next therapy session, when the contract must be renewed. If a client refuses to close his or her Escape Hatches at all, the therapist must consider, in supervision, whether it is appropriate to continue with therapy and whether the client should be admitted to hospital.

Contract Making

The making of a contract as described in Chapter 10 is, of course, an important therapeutic procedure in itself because it requires the client to think clearly about his problem and what it is he really wants to change. This might not be possible until decontamination work has been done and the client's Child ego state has been deconfused. Some of the techniques and procedures briefly described in this chapter might, in fact, be used in preparation for making an overall therapeutic contract. Each procedure will, of course, be the subject of a separate session contract or work agreement.

Listening

When a client first goes to see a therapist, he or she might or might not be ready to 'let it all spill out'. Often, I find, it has taken some people weeks, months, or even years, to pluck up the courage to come at all! Sometimes they need encouragement to get it said, but more often it is necessary to intervene from time to time with questions that will help the client stick to the point – especially when they might want to avoid the discomfort of revealing the very thing that troubles them most. Generally speaking, however, the first session is just a 'listening' session and I rarely write notes until after the client has gone.

An important element in the listening process is simply the giving of close attention to the client with appropriate – but not 'probing' – eye contact and the making of brief responses so that the client knows he has been heard. This is not a recommendation for 'grunt therapy' – although there are occasions when no more than 'uh-huh' or 'hm ...' is necessary. Occasionally to summarize what you have just heard the client say not only lets him know he has been heard and understood but gives opportunity to clarify or amplify anything that seems to need it.

History Taking

A Developmental History is an important diagnostic tool and often reveals experiences that led to the client's Early Script Decisions, or at least to reinforcing experiences that might have come later in life. I provide my clients with sheets which have a square for each year of their age and ask them to note (for homework between sessions) anything they believe to be emotionally significant that occurred at various ages, beginning with the circumstances of their birth. Writing what amounts to a mini-autobiography gets the client actively involved in the therapeutic process and frequently indicates (sometimes by its omissions!) areas for more detailed exploration. Sometimes, clients begin to ask their parents or older siblings about events in their childhood, whether or not they reveal that they are 'going for counselling'.

Frequently, the client does not complete the Developmental History in one go and might take it home a time or two to add further details. In any case, further details are often added during the course of counselling sessions. When the sheets seem reasonably complete, I usually begin work on them by asking the client to 'talk me through' what he has entered on them, drawing attention to whatever features he feels are probably of particular significance.

Background details of parents, siblings, partners, and other important players in the client's 'drama of life' need to be garnered, together with information about the mental and physical health, genetic or family predispositions, appetite and eating habits, sleep patterns and experience of dreams, etc.

Appendix C is the page of 'instructions' I give to the client together with a set of A4 sheets containing fifteen squares on each sheet, with the age (starting from 0) in the top left-hand corner.

Learning the TA Language

At the end of our first session I usually give my clients a copy of my own little book *Taking Charge of Your Own Life – A Brief Introduction to Transactional Analysis*[40] and suggest that they answer 'Some Questions to Ask Yourself'. This helps them not only to understand the TA concepts but to apply them to themselves. Looking together at their responses in later sessions provides an opportunity to clarify any misunderstandings and to enlarge as necessary. A similar but extended list of questions is included in this book in Appendix D. Learning the language of TA actually enables client and counsellor to say things to each other which might otherwise be virtually unsayable!

Early sessions, once the client has told her story, are often devoted to exploring how her present lifestyle and relationships are illuminated by an understanding of ego states, transactions, stroking, time-structuring, and game playing, etc. It is often possible at this stage to get some idea of the Script Messages, in terms of Injunctions and Drivers, which have led to Early Decisions and influenced the formation of the Script. Passivity can often be observed, identified, and confronted.

The Cathexis Approach

The work of Jaqui Schiff and her colleagues at the Cathexis Institute has already been referred to in Chapter 9. The Cathexis approach was developed primarily for the treatment of schizophrenia, and Jaqui Schiff 'adopted' young schizophrenics, aged between fifteen and thirty, into her own family and effectively brought them up all over again with a new set of 'Parent' messages.

This work was first developed in the United States, and later Jaqui Schiff established a residential treatment facility called *Athma Shakti Vidyalaya* in Bangalore, India. A similar facility has now operated for several years in Birmingham, England, under the direction of Jenny Robinson, and also in Denkendorf, Germany. The basic philosophy is that people behave as they do because they choose to do so, not because they can't help it. In principle, therefore, the person can decide to behave differently.

Five basic principles underlie the treatment programme.

1 Schizophrenics do significantly better in a highly structured environment where the behavioural boundaries are absolutely clear.

2 They need to know they can get a response to their behaviour; so there is continual confrontation from a caring position and a clear expectation that they will behave differently when appropriate.

3 The schizophrenic suffers from a 'crazy' Parent ego state because of developmental factors. The Parent ego state, therefore, may have to be de-cathected or 'switched off' before a reparenting process can begin. (Surprisingly, most clients can do this easily once they have decided to do it!)

4 In the reparenting phase the therapist becomes the client's effective parent, often being addressed by the client as Mum or Dad. Actual adoption has sometimes been undertaken. The reparenting process enables the client to get rid of an inappropriate frame of reference and replace it with new values and definitions of reality.

5 In some cases regressive work is undertaken when the client will re-experience earlier stages of childhood development that were not originally completed successfully. Clients in residence are taught practical tasks such as cooking, personal hygiene, etc. They learn that *problems are solvable* and they are taught how to solve them.[43]

The passive behaviours described in Chapter 9 are not associated exclusively with severe mental illnesses such as schizophrenia. The Cathexis Model has very wide application even in day-to-day life, especially for clients who have a character disorder or antisocial personality structure, as dealt with in Chapters 11 and 12. The goal of treatment is to get the client to *think* clearly and creatively about the problem and about possible solutions. Asking questions which are designed to elicit information (*not* critical challenges!) is usually a good way to mobilize the Adult ego state. Any discounting, especially failure to take account of what is actually going on, should be confronted. If there is agitation it is important to intervene before it escalates into incapacitation or violence, as already described in Chapter 9.

Discounting is a central feature of passivity and I would again refer the reader to *The Healthy Model* quoted on p. 35.

Process Therapy

Developed by clinical psychologist, Taibi Kahler, the Process Model provides a rapid means of assessing personality and communication style by careful observation of the five Drivers referred to in Chapter 8. The detection of Driver behaviours in the client points the way to the Script Process. The Driver puts a condition on the client's sense of OK-ness, so that he will feel 'I'm OK *if* I am perfect' – or if I 'try hard' or am 'strong' or 'please people' or 'hurry up'. But for each of the Drivers there is an Allower that can function as an antidote, and the therapeutic process aims at establishing these alternative 'messages'. Petruska Clarkson has pointed out the need to distinguish between the 'oppressing messages' conveyed by the Drivers and the 'values which are aspired to in the *Physis* sense of a "general creative force"'.[31]

As already mentioned in Chapter 8, an account of Process Therapy can be found in Stewart and Joines's book *TA To-day*, as well as other books and articles.[19, 20, 21]

Because the Driver comes from the parents' Parent ego state and not from their Child, the motivation behind it might not be parental self-interest, as it is with the Injunction (which comes from the parents' Child). It might be that experience has convinced Mother or Father that it is in the youngster's best interests to accept these conditions of OK-ness. As with the Counter-injunction the intention is good but with the Driver the consequence can be toxic!

Dream Work

The interpretation of dreams, in the Freudian or Jungian sense, is not a feature of transactional analysis although some practitioners with appropriate training might use such an approach. TA psychotherapists and counsellors are more likely to use a Gestalt approach to working with dreams. This starts from the premise that every element in the dream, animate and inanimate, represents some feature of the dreamer's self. The client is invited to tell and retell the dream from the point of view of these different elements, identifying with them, one at a time, and then dialoguing between one and another, inventing missing elements and, perhaps, even making up a different ending to the dream.

I have found that this way of using dreams almost invariably helps the client to gain significant insights into their own emotional processes and often results in constructive change, even when the client is not consciously aware of the significance of what is happening. For example, 'Chris' dreamed that he was coming out of the factory where he worked and was stopped by a security guard who accused him of stealing gold. He is taken before the boss who agrees not to prosecute if he will admit the theft. 'Chris' first told the dream as he wished. Then he retold it in the present tense, as if it was happening now. I then asked him to say which ego state he was in as 'himself' in the dream and he said Adapted Child. Next he 'became' the security guard and declared himself to be in his Parent ego state. He went back to being himself in Child and I asked him who the security guard reminded him of and he said, of course, 'My dad'. In a fairly prolonged piece of work, he identified first with himself in Child and then with his dad in Parent, experiencing the feelings and thoughts of each as the dialogue unfolded. He declared his demand to be free to live his own life in his own way, and heard his father, through his own replay, acknowledge his right to do this. The outcome was that 'Chris' was thereafter better able to make decisions for himself and he began to have warmer and more positive memories of his dad, who had died many years before.

Obviously, there are many other ways of using dreams in therapy. The use of ego states is, of course, a characteristically TA way of working but is not essential. A method similar to that briefly described above is described in detail by Fritz Perls in *Gestalt Therapy Verbatim*,[36] which is a transcript of his talks and actual therapeutic work in a dream workshop. For anyone just embarking on the use of dream work this is an excellent text to begin with.

Uses of Imagery

The human capacity to make mental images is not restricted to our dream life alone. Images we make in normal waking life and in fantasy are often metaphors for memories, objects, people, or experiences that, for reasons which might remain obscure, we do not deal with objectively. To access these metaphors can be a powerful means of gaining insight into a problem and into our inner resources for dealing with it. An excellent book, for anyone who wishes to explore this approach, is Dina Glauberman's *Life Choices and Life Changes Through Image Work*.[44]

A method I have found helpful with clients who are reasonably imaginative I call 'Imagery with Notes' – for want of a better name. I was introduced to it at a conference of counsellors years ago and do not know whom to thank for it. But it works somewhat as described below.

Ask the client first to settle down comfortably and, if it seems helpful, perhaps do a brief relaxation exercise. Often I do no more than ask him to take three deep breaths, hold them briefly, and say, as he breathes out, the words 'Re ... lax ... and ... let ... go', making the words use up the whole lungful of air. Relaxing the body relaxes the mind and facilitates communication with the unconscious.

Have a prepared sheet with the following questions on it and, as the client answers them and reveals his imagery, write down what he says.

1   What problem are you aiming to resolve?

2   What are your strengths?

3   Make an image which represents your strengths and describe it to me. (The image might be, for example, a lion or a steel girder.)

4   What is the purpose of your life? What are you here for?

5   Make an image to represent your life's purpose. (He might image, for example, an obstacle course or a sack race.)

6   How do you prevent yourself from fulfilling your own purpose?

7   Make an image which represents how you sabotage yourself and describe it to me.

8   If you were free to do exactly as you please, what would you do or be?

9   Make an image which represents your free choice of being and describe it to me.

10 What clues do you now have to the solution of the problem you declared at the beginning?

I then give the client the completed sheet and ask them to reflect on their answers and to bring the sheet back to the next session for possible further work.

The above account is, of course, only a brief outline. Practitioners experienced in metaphor work, and those who have read

Glauberman's book or something similar, might make a great deal of use of each image as it is revealed.

Racket System Analysis

This approach, developed by Richard Erskine and Marilyn Zalcman,[13] and mentioned in Chapter 6, depends on the recognition of Script Beliefs about Self, Others, and the Quality of Life. These beliefs are manifested in a variety of 'Rackety Displays', – that is, different manifestations of the Scripty belief system that was established in childhood, including Observable Behaviours, Reported Internal Experiences – aches and pains, dizziness, or palpitations, for example – and Fantasies, frequently of the worst thing that could happen and, possibly, of the best. As these manifestations occur, they are remembered by the person who then uses the memories to reinforce the original Script Beliefs. So a self-perpetuating Racket System is set up. The therapeutic process calls for a variety of techniques and interventions designed to break into this vicious circle and to provide positive new experiences that are incompatible with the Script Beliefs. Treatment interventions suggested by Erskine and Zalcman include, for example, identifying needs and asking for them to be met; behaving in a more sociable manner to experience positive responses from people; changing fantasies of being rejected and unloved to fantasies of being loved and valued; and learning to express underlying and authentic feelings. These new experiences can then be remembered and will reinforce a new system of beliefs that are life enhancing. A technique for engaging with the client's true feelings which underlie the Racket Feelings is described in Chapter 6 on p. 38.

The use of Racket System Analysis is well described by Ian Stewart in *Transactional Analysis Counselling in Action.*[45]

Parenting, Reparenting, and Self-reparenting

While the practitioners of some styles of therapy and counselling might adopt a relatively detached Adult stance in relation to their clients, the transactional analyst will use whatever ego state he or she feels is appropriate and helpful to the achievement of the client's goals. Parental interventions might include support and reassurance, exhortation and persuasion, as well as the Potency, Permission, and Protection referred to below. There are certain circumstances, however, when I feel it appropriate to provide Parenting in a more structured way, perhaps over an extended period. This might be, for example, when the client demonstrates a character-disorder problem arising from a weak or deficient Parent ego state and fails to provide Care or Control either for himself or for others who might be dependent on him. Social workers and probation officers and some teachers will be familiar with this situation. I might then ask the client if he or she will agree to a Parenting Contract, that is an explicit Adult agreement that the therapist will take a specific parent-type role in relation to the client for the duration of the contract. This does not, of course, preclude the therapist from using Adult or Child ego states with the client when appropriate, any more than it would with a parent and their real grown-up son or daughter. Many character-disordered clients will not, of course, enter readily into a Parenting Contract. While they will receive the Care with enthusiasm they are likely to resist or resent the Control. Nevertheless, exploring such a contract idea with them is usually well worth while and can lead to the client's gaining more insight into his or her real needs even if it is not possible to establish a contract formally,

Parenting Contracts, whether formal or informal, can be very demanding on client and on therapist. The Control element would require us to deal with beliefs and values and issues of right and wrong which some practitioners might consider entirely outside their remit. The Care element would require me to respond to the client's need for affection, encouragement and interest, and to share his joys and his sorrows. Above all, I would give him or her permission – when I sensed they were ready for it – to function autonomously and independently of me, as a growing son or daughter would expect.

The Parenting Contract rests on the belief that *Physis*, the growth force of nature, depends upon parental nourishment if it is to ensure the client's growth and his capacity to 'take the happiness of others into consideration'[22] – that is, if he is to become a functional member of society. Such nourishment requires both Care and Control and, under a Parenting Contract, it is the therapist's responsibility to provide this two-fold nourishment. The details of the contract must be carefully thought through and agreed by both parties 'in Adult', and should be set down in writing, perhaps even signed and dated. Whether it is appropriate for a counsellor, as distinct from a psychotherapist, to contract for treatment of this kind is a matter each practitioner must decide for him- or herself after discussion in supervision.

The Reparenting process has been referred to above under the heading of 'The Cathexis Approach' and is a very specialized form of treatment. Self-reparenting, however, is a kind of self-therapy the client may be encouraged to pursue on his own initiative. I often suggest that a client buys Muriel James's book *It's Never Too Late to be*

Happy – The Psychology of Self-Reparenting.[46] This is a work-book that includes many exercises the client can do in his own time. As he comes across issues of particular relevance to his own circumstances he can bring them up in the therapy session. I find this is a particularly useful way of getting clients actively involved in their own therapy.

Three Ps

Practitioners should note that there are three essential principles of clinical practice in transactional analysis. They are Potency, Permission, and Protection. Potency refers to the therapist's power and effectiveness in overcoming the negative or destructive messages from parents and others that have been restricting the client's potential for living. To do this the therapist must give the client permission to disobey these Script messages. Permission means a licence for the client to give up some behaviour because he can see that it is dysfunctional. This can be quite threatening for the client who might need assurance that he has the protection of the therapist while he makes changes in the way he thinks, feels, and behaves, and that he can call on the therapist in times of need. There are many ways in which the therapist can protect his client, and it might be important that he is available, perhaps by telephone, at particularly critical times during the course of therapy.

The use of Potency and Protection and the Permission Transaction, is described by Southey Swede in *How to Cure.*[47] Unfortunately, this account of 'How Eric Berne Practised Transactional Analysis' is now out of print so readers might find it helpful to have a brief résumé of the four stages of the Permission Transaction that Swede describes as Potency, Permission, Protection, and Re-inforcement. They are as follows:

1 Potency
(a) Hook the client's Adult, or wait until it is active.
(b) Form an alliance with the client's Adult.
(c) State your plan and see if the client's Adult agrees with it.

2 Permission
If all is clear, give the client's Child permission to disobey his Parent ego state with no 'ifs', 'ands', or 'buts'.

3 Protection
Offer the client's Child protection from the consequences of disobedience.

4 Reinforcement
Reinforce the permission by assuring the client's Adult that it is all right.

This account is taken from Southey Swede's book which uses the Basic Ego State Model illustrated in Figure 2 on p. 8 of this book. In the light of the New Ego State Model, of course, the 'Parent' in the account given by Swede might be the Parent-in-the-Child of Mother or Father, which the client needs permission to disobey. Readers should note, of course, that the above procedure is more properly a feature of psychotherapy than of counselling, using the distinctions described earlier.

Many Other Methods and Techniques

There are, of course, many other methods and techniques a practitioner can use. The ones referred to above represent only a small selection of those I might use myself. Others are, for example, journaling, behavioural techniques and self-control programmes, desensitization, relaxation, stress management and Neuro-Linguistic Programming (NLP), and other techniques associated with, for example, psychosynthesis, to mention but a few.

One of the attractions of TA is that it is compatible with most other styles of counselling and psychotherapy. Not only does this mean that the practitioner using transactional analysis can call upon a wide variety of techniques from other therapies to enhance his work, but also that practitioners of other therapies can call upon the insights of transactional analysis for the benefit of *their* clients.

Supervision

Relate counsellors, social workers, probation officers, and many other professionals are familiar with supervision as a normal requirement for those who help others deal with the problems of living. The British Association for Counselling requires contractual supervisory arrangements as a condition of accreditation. But supervision does not mean that the counsellor or psychotherapist must have some 'superior' person keeping an eye on him to ensure that he is behaving in an acceptably professional manner. It is designed to ensure that the counsellor, who shares so many burdens with his clients, is not working in isolation but has support from a colleague, and in particular (as mentioned at the beginning of this chapter) to ensure that he is not sucked into emotional overinvolvement – which one of my teachers many years ago described as 'a gruesome twosome'!

The supervisor will frequently suggest ideas the therapist has not thought of or has not explored, and the two will bounce ideas off each other as they search for the best way of helping the client. Also, they might explore how the process between the therapist and the client can sometimes be reflected in what happens between the supervisor and the therapist. So supervision is designed to help and protect the therapist and the client; and it is, of course, of immense value to every supervisor, too, who learns from his supervisees.

The United Kingdom Council on Psychotherapy does not, at present, demand contractual supervision as a condition of registration. There is an expectation, however, that professional members of the Institute of Transactional Analysis, through which registration is channelled, will make proper arrangements for supervision on their own account. Group or peer supervision, with one or more colleagues, is often the most practical and inexpensive way to meet this requirement. There is no necessary expectation that the supervisor should be more advanced than the supervisee but obviously he or she should be widely experienced.

Part Three:
A Spiritual Perspective

14 The Total Human Being

The Creative Child

In clinical practice – and equally in other fields of transactional analysis – it is a primary goal to engage with that marvellously energetic, creative, curious, adventurous Child-in-the-Child which is the well-spring of human spiritual growth – by which I mean the growth of *the whole person in relationship*, the total human being. This Child, if richly nurtured by good parenting, is the seed from which the total human being can, in ideal circumstances, emerge. It is puzzling that intelligence and the power of reason should so often be regarded as the essential criterion of humanness because many of the 'higher' animals display some degree of intelligence and often quite a lot! The one attribute that human beings possess *exclusively*, however, is creative imagination, though intelligence is undoubtedly an element of it. This creativity is vested in the Child ego state.

The first purpose of every newborn child is simply to survive. And because he *must* grow and mature to survive beyond the stage of immediate dependency on mother, growth will normally follow in the ordinary course of events. The essential characteristic of this survivor is self-interest. But in his innate wisdom, every child knows that he cannot survive in the final analysis and serve his *own* interests without taking into account the interests of others, especially his parents.

A Being-in-Community

But not only his parents. This child is part of a living organism, and his own life depends on his participation in it. In the beginning, the organism is just himself and his mother; later, as he becomes aware of his father, it is his nuclear family. Sadly, in these days of 'Families without Fatherhood'[32] there are many children who lack that resource for life unless they can find it in a father substitute. The days of extended families, to which each individual 'belonged', are rapidly declining so it is increasingly difficult for the growing child to experience that nourishment which Berne recognized as providing the 'urge to grow and behave "better" – that is, in accordance with principles ... which take the happiness of others into consideration'.[22]

As John Donne put it, 'No man is an Island, entire of it self'. And so there is a profound sense in which the child – in due course an adult – might not really be alive at all, at least not spiritually, except in relationship with others. He is a member of a community that is a living organism, not just dependent on it but also committed to it, because it is dependent on him. Apart from his co-operative participation in this organism he will die, psychologically and spiritually, whatever happens to him biologically. In the days of open fires, a log or a coal would burn brightly so long as it remained in the fire and was a contributory part of it. But, if you removed it from the fire with tongs and placed it on the hearth, it would die out in minutes or even seconds. Similarly, an individual wilfully separated from the living community-organism will die spiritually as surely as a finger, severed from the physical body, will die unless it is stitched back on quickly, otherwise no amount of surgery will then restore it to 'life'. This is why the giving and receiving of Strokes, which Steiner called 'the unit of human love',[4] is essential if, as Berne put it, the spinal cord is not to shrivel up! Strokes – Positive Strokes, that is – are a manifestation of living spirit.

Autonomy and Aspiration

It is from our interaction with others that the human spirit arises. Without such interaction there *is* no spirit. You cannot have a team spirit, a school spirit, or a party spirit without a team, a school, or a party. It is within the group that the spirit is generated and it is from the group that the spirit proceeds and flows, even if the group consists of only two persons. And so we cannot truly know ourselves as persons until we are truly known by someone else, be it a parent, a lover, a God, or a counsellor!

Curiously, the goal of transactional analysis to promote Autonomy in the individual can be counterproductive in spiritual terms if, as might sometimes happen, Autonomy is taken to mean total independence and self-sufficiency. One dictionary definition of 'autonomy' is 'Freedom to determine one's own actions, behaviour, etc.'. And philosophically, it means 'the doctrine that the individual human will is governed only by its own principles and laws'.[7] But autonomy in transactional analysis is the capacity for Intimacy, Spontaneity, and Awareness, and these qualities imply relationship rather than total self-sufficiency. Independence from the constraints of our Scripts is, of course, crucially important for personal fulfilment but a person who is entirely independent of the influence of other people in the real world of here and now, with commitment to no one but himself, is not a total human being of body, mind, and spirit. He cannot be because the spirit manifests in relationship. In the final analysis such a person will know only loneliness, isolation, and forsakenness, no matter what personal achievement he has aspired to! I am reminded of a song sung by the Kings Singers which goes 'You're building a wall to surround yourself, you're building a wall to protect yourself, you're building a wall to defend yourself – You're building a wall that will break your heart!'

Physis, Berne tells us, 'takes the happiness of others into consideration'. M. Scott Peck recognizes this in defining 'real love' as 'the will to extend oneself for the purpose of nurturing one's own or another's spiritual growth'.[34]

What *is* Spiritual?

The word 'spiritual' is being widely used today in counselling and psychotherapy circles, usually without any implication of institutional religion, and it no doubt means different things to different people. According to *Collins English Dictionary*,[7] the word 'spiritual' can be used in several different ways. One of them is, 'relating to or characteristic of sacred things, the church, religion, etc.'. But that meaning is not relevant to our present discussion. Neither is it helpful for counsellors and psychotherapists to think of 'spiritual' in terms of the paranormal, even if the phenomena invoked appear, on the face of it, to be good and in the interests of the client's well-being. If anything paranormal is implied, then words such as 'psychic' or even 'occult' might be more appropriate. In a world sick of cynicism and desperate for something to believe in, this distinction should help to avoid confusion with things that are, or might be, 'out of this world'. This is not a question of whether paranormal experiences are genuine realities which are merely outside the remit of conventional science. It is a matter of whether there is a relationship, within which a spirit or attitude is generated and from which that spirit flows to embrace others in loving and creative harmony. I would expect to find such a spirit, at least potentially, in a TA therapy group, a marriage, a church, or even a football team – but not, as a colleague once suggested, at a rock concert! Spirit, I believe, flows from mutually supportive relationships that have a common creative purpose (in a rock band, perhaps, or a symphony orchestra), but not from mere corporate self-indulgence.

The human spirit is sometimes defined as 'the core self'; it is the essential 'heart' of the individual that seeks liberation and fulfilment through counselling, psychotherapy, and some religions and philosophies. But the 'core self' can no more manifest in creative *spiritual* growth than, say, a living biological sperm can manifest in creative *biological* growth unless it is united in intimate relationship with a living biological ovum. Whether spiritually or biologically, relationship is essential to growth.

An alternative meaning of 'spiritual' is 'standing in a relationship based on communication between the souls or minds of the persons involved',[7] This is not paranormal; it is an entirely normal and familiar feature of everyday experience. As such it is well within the remit of practitioners using transactional analysis, whether the 'persons involved' are past or present, visible or invisible, because transactional analysis is about the analysis of transactions, or working out what's going on between people.

We must recognize, of course, that some of the 'people' exist now only in our own heads. They are the images and memories, and the persistent recorded voices of people we depended on for our survival in our infancy. And we still hear those voices now in grown-up life and sometimes still respond to them, in our relationships with here-and-now people, as if our survival depended on them even yet. And it does not – not, at any rate, if the persistent voices come from the often toxic Parent-in-the-Child of our Mothers and Fathers which, when it all turns out, is simply our parents looking after themselves in the interests of *their* survival!

The Therapeutic Relationship

In the therapeutic situation the two most important people are the client and the therapist, between whom there is a very special kind of communication going on that can, I believe, appropriately be called spiritual. The purpose of the therapeutic relationship is healing and growth, and this happens – if it happens at all – *through* the relationship, regardless of whether the practitioner is a transactional analyst, a psychoanalyst, a Gestaltist, a person-centred counsellor, or a practitioner of any other 'school'. And the healing and the growth are for the client *and* for the therapist. No therapist is entirely 'whole' and in no need of a physician. For this reason we do not practise without regular supervision, even after we are qualified. So healing and growth for the therapist happens within the supervisory relationship and also within the therapeutic relationship. As Jung has said, 'The meeting of two personalities is like the contact of two chemical substances; if there is any reaction, both are transformed'.[48]

Living in Two Worlds

There is, however, a third usage of the word 'spiritual'. This is 'relating to spirit or soul and not to physical nature or matter'.[7] So I also use the word 'spiritual' to mean our human capacity to distinguish good from evil, right from wrong, just from unjust, truth from falsehood, and the wholesome from the unwholesome – among other opposites. These categories of thought are quite distinct from 'physical nature or matter', even though the manifestation of, say, evil or injustice might well be clearly objective and concrete; and 'spirit' is certainly concerned with issues of right and wrong, justice, truth, etc.

To acknowledge the spiritual dimension of life, therefore, is simply to recognize that there is more to life than meets the eye, that we live in two worlds: the world of nature, which has to do with self-interest and sensual pleasure; and the world of spirit, which has to do with loving relationships and with self-giving. These two dimensions of human life are not mutually exclusive. For a total human being they are two sides of the same coin. The mind or soul (Greek: *psyche*) provides an interface between the body and the spirit. No counsellor or psychotherapist (and the latter word means 'doctor of souls') can heal the total human being unless he takes the human spirit into account, recognizing the spirit as a manifestation of love flowing from a relationship between people.

Spirituality is characterized by an attitude towards ourselves and others in which there is a willingness to forego immediate gratification in favour of some ultimate good, of benefit to the living organism or community we are a part of. Genuine spirituality, which is non-exploitative, might be represented in transactional analysis by *Physis*, the 'growth force of nature which', Berne observed, 'makes organisms evolve into higher forms, embryos grow into adults, sick people get better and healthy people strive to attain their ideals' and which 'takes the happiness of others into consideration'.[22] It is, I think, confusing and apparently inconsistent with this that, in his original Script diagram in *What Do You Say After You Say Hello?* Berne defined the Arrow of Aspiration with the words 'I want it my own way'.[5] He was, of course, writing in the 1960s when a new spirit of liberation was at last emerging after thousands of years of parental restraint during which human beings had struggled to survive as individuals while trying to keep other people's rules. The old morality was being questioned and sometimes rejected altogether. 'Doing one's own thing' was the criterion of autonomy, rather than the capacity for Intimacy, Spontaneity, and Awareness. But perhaps, in the midst of all this, Berne recognized that 'my own way', uncontaminated by Script influences, is indeed a way that 'takes the happiness of others into consideration'. This is, I believe, the natural disposition of a script-free human being.

In Jung's analytical psychology, a power for good, comparable in some respects with *Physis*, is represented by the Collective Unconscious. Jung (unlike Freud) saw the unconscious mind as containing not only repressed material but also a vast storehouse of inherited wisdom that we share with all humankind and through which, he believed, we may come into contact with God.[48] This spiritual nature of the total human being manifests in loving relationship and in true community.

More recently, biologist, Rupert Sheldrake,[49] has considered the concept of 'morphic fields' to account for many phenomena that cannot be adequately explained by the current understandings of conventional science. Sheldrake draws on the notion of 'forms' that can be found in the philosophies of Socrates and Plato. Each 'form' or 'idea', they believed, existed as a kind of pattern or mould that defined what was eternal and unchangeable in nature and also what was eternal and unchangeable in morals and society. Such ideas are, perhaps, not far removed from religious ideas of God, which some people are uncomfortable with, often because of their association with institutional religion. But we might do well to remember the fundamental belief of Alcoholics Anonymous (and many derivative 'anonymous' groups) in 'a power greater than ourselves'. AA caters for all sorts and conditions of men and women – atheists, agnostics, and believers – but few who know their work would question that they are among the most successful of all therapeutic group movements!

Living Planet

The astonishing speed of development in the field of communication in recent years has led us to think of the world as a 'global village'. Our social interdependency is relatively easy to recognize at the level of the nuclear, or even the extended, family; but no intelligent person, aware of the world scene, can fail to recognize that interdependency extends now to the whole of humanity, even the whole of nature. The notion of Earth as a living planet did not begin with James Lovelock's Gaia hypothesis but he has done much to help us accept that we have a responsibility not only for the happiness of one another but also for the harmony and balance of the entire ecological environment we live in. Lovelock observes that 'the evolution of the species of organisms is not independent of the evolution of their material environment. Indeed the species and their environment are tightly coupled and evolve as a single system.' 'The greater part of our own environment on Earth', Lovelock comments, 'is always perfect and comfortable for life.'[50]

Nature is self-regulating. A damaged environment, a damaged body, a damaged mind, have within themselves the resources for self-healing. If the damage is severe, of course, healing might not take place without the assistance of the environmentalist, the physician, or the psychotherapist. And, if the damage is excessive, it might be beyond healing altogether and the organism will die. But the natural propensity is always for healing, for a return to a perfectly balanced and harmonious state, provided that the organism is alive.

Perfect Wholeness

But there is a perfection to which the whole of humanity aspires collectively. We are members of a community-organism the essential purpose of which is to live together in harmony with one another and with our environment. Our individual and our communal well-being are dependent on the harmony and balance of nature; and our natural environment is equally dependent on us to nurture it with love and respect and without exploitation. So the analysis of transactions might not stop at working out what's going on between people but could also take account of what's going on between people and the environment.

It was Victorian writer and scientist, Henry Drummond, who drew particular attention to *Natural Law in the Spiritual World*[51] in his book of that title. An example from the experience of every student in the physics lab is the behaviour of iron filings in response to a magnetic field. Bar magnets were handed out and a piece of paper laid over the top. Iron filings were then sprinkled on to the paper and they were seen to form themselves into a beautiful and entirely predictable pattern, following the lines of magnetic force. The iron filings had no alternative but to behave as nature demanded. Human behaviour, however, is governed not by natural laws but by moral laws that are not inherent in our genes. They are, nevertheless, passed on from parents and others to children – if they are transmitted at all. Unlike the iron filings, we have the freedom to defy them. Evolutionary theory and social philosophy have, perhaps, called in question any notion of unchanging absolutes such as the

'forms' that were central to Plato's theory of ideas; but more immediate human experience of the social realities of here and now must
give pause for thought. Arnold Beisser has observed that 'For the first
time in the history of mankind, man finds himself in a position
where, rather than needing to adapt himself to an existing order, he
must be able to adapt himself to a series of changing orders'.[52] It is
against this background of a world in a state of flux, in which the
notion of 'absolutes' of any kind has been largely rejected, that the
caseworker, counsellor, and psychotherapist must work, striving to
help the confused client make some sense out of the chaos. But the
indisputable fact is that when the ancient rules are broken, suffering
invariably follows, either for the rule breaker or for others whose
happiness he has not taken into consideration.

The Value of Suffering

M. Scott Peck, in *The Road Less Travelled*,[34] gives one of his chapters
the curious title 'The Healthiness of Depression', pointing out that it
is the experience of depression – the roots of which might have been
established in infancy – that finally drives the sufferer to a therapist
and he begins at last to address the underlying problem and to open
up the possibility of a new and healthier direction in life. But in a
similar sort of way there is, in principle, a fundamental 'healthiness'
in all suffering, though this might be difficult to acknowledge when
the suffering is intense and prolonged. All suffering presents us with
a crisis that demands a resolution. Ideally, there follows a search for
healing, harmony, wholeness, and freedom from pain. But it is spiritual rather than physical or even mental pain that is now at issue. In
that context, suffering can be a real growth experience because it is
suffering that tells us that something is wrong, that there is some dis-
ease calling for healing; and suffering is the first stage in Allen
Wheelis's sequence leading to change, as described at the beginning
of Chapter 13. This sequence, incidentally, describes the process of
healing, not only in the individual but also in relationships and in
organizations of all kinds, where there is dis-ease and a failure to
function as a healthy organism should. The organization might be,
for example, a marriage, a family, a school, a church, a business, or
a government – local, national, or international.
    The value of suffering, as Jung recognized, is not that it provides
yet another opportunity to learn how to avoid it in future, but that it
provides opportunity to learn how to face it and endure it, quickly
and effectively. Once this has been done, we can move on to the next
crisis with its further opportunities for spiritual growth.

There are, of course, many people in the community who do not themselves suffer but who are a cause of suffering to others. These are the character-disordered people dealt with in Chapters 11 and 12, and who have relatively little disposition 'to take the happiness of others into consideration'.[22] Their antisocial behaviour does not necessarily amount to crime, which is just one, perhaps extreme, manifestation of character disorder. Nevertheless, it commonly involves a breach of the generally accepted norm for morally acceptable behaviour in that particular society. The problem for us, however, as Beisser indicated in the quotation above, is that the 'norm' to which people are expected or required to conform, is becoming increasingly unclear.

The relative indifference of character disordered people to the suffering of others means, as we have already noted, that they often do very well for themselves individually in business or profession but are frequently unsuccessful in establishing the kind of committed, loving relationships from which spiritual growth arises. They enjoy little if any real community spirit and no intimate fellowship with others. They live in one world only – the world of self. Neurotics, on the other hand, are likely to be not only over-responsible but also overdependent – often overdependent on other people being dependent on them!

Spiritual Survival

Our survival – our spiritual survival, that is, as total human beings, able and willing to distinguish between good and evil and to choose accordingly – depends on the authentic Nurturing Parent voice that Cares and Controls and that might, perhaps, have something to do with what Christians understand by 'the fatherhood of God'. Even Freud acknowledged that the superego's function of 'limiting satisfactions' of the Id, is one of the foundations on which the structure of civilized life is built.[28] The authentic Parent ego state, incorporating Care and Control, is the distilled essence of thousands of years of human experience, passed on from generation to generation. It *knows* what works and what doesn't, what's 'right' and what's 'wrong' – not just for the self-interested survivor but for the total living organism, the community, of which he is an interdependent part. And that knowledge is, and always has been, *common* knowledge in all cultures throughout history, regardless of religion, with relatively little variation from one culture to another.

Only in the comfort and security of parental nurture can the Natural Child, born as nature intended it to be, respond to the 'growth force of nature' within itself, developing whatever skills it needs to fulfil its own potential, whether it works with wood or computers, microscopes or pneumatic drills, musical instruments, people, or any other medium of work and creativity.

To set about analysing our Ego States, our Transactions, our Games and our Scripts to work out what is *really* going on, and to make whatever changes are appropriate, is not nearly so awesome a task as it might at first appear. It is a realistic option for anyone willing to give the time and commitment to it. Many, who are aware of their own needs, can do as much as is necessary without a counsellor or therapist, using such work-books as Stewart and Joines's *TA To-day*,[21] James and Jongeward's *Born to Win*[53] or Muriel James's *It's Never Too Late to be Happy*.[46] Others will need a skilled practitioner, who will be both counsellor and friend, to work with them. Not everyone, of course, will be willing to do this, either with or without a counsellor. Many people will prefer to rub along with a familiar repertoire of Games and Rackets, guaranteed to maintain a Script which is comfortable precisely because of its familiarity. Life as it is might be reasonably congenial, even fun – though the fun is likely to be at someone else's expense! The challenge of spiritual growth is often simply too much bother, and many will choose to leave things as they are. As a client once said to me, 'I can't be pestered'!

Berne wrote in the last sentence of *Games People Play*,[2] that perhaps 'there is no hope for the human race; but there is hope for individual members of it'. We can, therefore, choose to be among the 'individual members' of this community-organism, sharing the spiritual life enjoyed by others who have also made that choice. And for many, who have previously been committed to getting whatever they can out of life with only a minimum regard for the happiness of others, such a choice can be the first, life-transforming step in finding a new direction.

Appendix A
For Advanced Practitioners and Trainees in Transactional Analysis

This appendix highlights the confusion and inconsistency that have long prevailed in our understanding of the structure and function of ego states – the very building blocks of which transactional analysis is constructed! It is offered to advanced practitioners and trainees as the rationale for my using, in this book, the New Ego State Model, which presents structure and function in one diagram. Practitioners who do not feel obligated to follow in the footsteps of mainstream convention will, I trust, find the New Ego State Model useful and this appendix interesting; but it might be confusing or even meaningless to those new to TA and unfamiliar with the conventions!

Readers who have read the mainstream literature will know that Eric Berne, and most later TA writers, used one model to illustrate the structural analysis of ego states, and a different model for functional analysis. The New Ego State Model used in this book, however, follows the example of Claude Steiner,[4] one of Berne's early associates, using just one diagram to illustrate structure and function. This is justified on the grounds that all structures have functions anyway, because an ego state is 'a way of thinking, feeling and behaving' – that is, it is functional. In fact, as demonstrated in Chapter 2, the function of ego states grows *out of* their structure. The diagram used in this book, however, is not the same as Steiner's but is redesigned in a way that I believe is more logical, more useful for practitioners wishing to use TA in casework and counselling (as opposed to radical psychotherapy), and simpler than trying to accommodate a variety of structural and functional models that are not even consistent with one another! I have used the New Ego State Model with clients for many years, and we have found it a clear and simple way of communicating with each other about what, in ego state terms, is going on. A selection of the many ego state diagrams appearing in the literature is discussed briefly below.

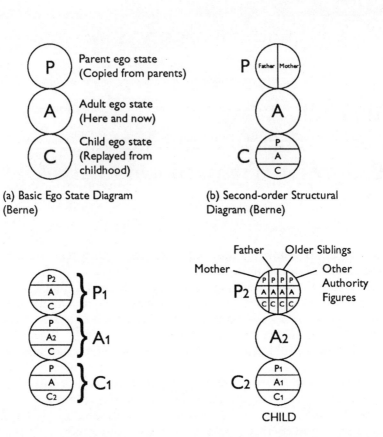

(a) Basic Ego State Diagram
(Berne)

(b) Second-order Structural
Diagram (Berne)

(c) Complete Second-order
Structural Analysis (Berne)

(d) Second-order Structural
Analysis (Woollams and Brown)

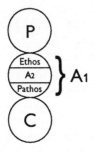

(e) Second-order Structure
of the Adult (Berne)

Figure 11 Structural Diagrams

Diagrams Used in Structural Analysis (Figure 11)

Figure 11(a): This is the simple 'first-order' basic ego state diagram used in Chapter 1 that has always been used for both structural and functional diagramming.

Figure 11(b): This 'second-order' structural diagram appears in Berne's *What Do You Say After You Say Hello?*[5] It includes the two Parent components usually derived from Father and Mother and the 'primitive' Parent, Adult and Child components already fixated in a youngster by the age of about five. However, in this diagram the ego states first observed on analysis (the 'first order' Basic Ego State Model) and those uncovered on more detailed analysis later (the 'second order' and more primitive ego states which actually came first developmentally!) are not numbered.

Figure 11(c): This diagram, which Berne calls 'complete second order structural analysis', appears in his *Transactional Analysis in Psychotherapy*.[3] The 'first order' or 'larger' ego states are labelled P1, A1 and C1 (although today's convention labels them P2, A2 and C2); and the finer subdivisions in each ego state are labelled P2, A2 and C2, which again differs from the current practice.

Figure 11(d): This diagram is how Woollams and Brown[16] present their understanding of second-order structural analysis, following current practice in numbering the ego states. This diagram is very similar to one used by Stewart and Joines.[21] Recognition is given to the variety of sources from which the Parent ego state is constructed. For advanced students and practitioners of TA using Redecision Therapy or a Script Analysis approach, this much more detailed understanding of the Parent ego state structure is important. The 'larger' ego states are here labelled P2, A2, and C2, as on the New Ego State Model. This style of labelling has now become standard practice.

Figure 11(e): Berne's diagram for the 'second order structure of the Adult', also appears in *Transactional Analysis in Psychotherapy*,[3] and actually combines structure and function as Berne speculates about his embryonic concept of the 'integrated Adult'. 'The mechanism of "integration"', he says, 'remains to be elucidated but it can be observed that certain people, when functioning *qua* Adult, have a charm and openness of nature which is reminiscent of that exhibited by children ... On the other hand there are moral qualities which are universally expected of people who undertake grown up responsibilities ... In this sense the Adult can be said to have child-like and ethical aspects ... transactionally, this means that anyone *functioning* [my italics] as an Adult should ideally exhibit three kinds of tendencies: personal attractiveness and responsiveness, objective data processing and ethical responsibility.'[3]

A comparable representation of the 'integrated Adult' is included in the New Ego State Model, showing, on the basis of Berne's own diagram, how function arises *from* structure. These qualities in the Adult are particularly relevant to the treatment of character problems, as Berne points out. Recognition of this is, perhaps, more important now than it was in Berne's day, in view of the changing social climate in which character problems are much more likely to arise as a result of inadequate or inappropriate parenting, as opposed to the relatively oppressive or restrictive parenting of the past.

Diagrams Used in Functional Analysis (Figure 12)

Figure 12(a) is the functional diagram in general use, as presented by Stewart and Joines[21] and others. As I pointed out in Chapter 2, however, it is, in my view, inappropriate to present the Parent ego state divisions (CP and NP) and the Child ego states divisions (AC and FC) in the same diagram because they represent different *kinds* of alternatives. In actual practice, controlling and nurturing (or caring) are two entirely compatible aspects of parental responsibility which might, in many situations, manifest both at the same time, while Free Child and Adapted Child behaviours are generally incompatible alternatives.

Figure 12(b) is Berne's own functional diagram, which appears in his last book, *What Do You Say After You Say Hello?*[5] In this diagram, Berne perceives the rebellious aspect of the Child ego state as distinct from the Natural (or Free) Child and the Adapted Child. Rebelliousness, however, can itself be a mode of adaptation to the voices of parents, just as are procrastination, compliance, and withdrawal, among other possible behaviours.

In the same book Berne recognized an element in the Child ego state which he called The Demon. His description of this element, which he named 'Jeder', suggests freedom from parental restraint, rather than adaptation to it. In fact, Berne even suggests that 'if the parents make friends with it, it will go on to later mischief ... ',[5] implying permission to be rebellious! It might be that the effective 'parent' for many people is neither Mother, Father, nor Older Siblings, but 'Other authority figures' [*See* Figure 11(d)]. Significant among these are powerful peer-group influences that often provide a blanket permission to do 'what everybody does'!

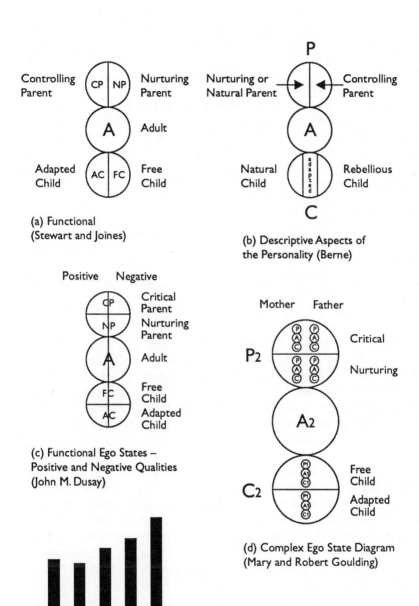

(a) Functional
(Stewart and Joines)

(b) Descriptive Aspects of
the Personality (Berne)

(c) Functional Ego States –
Positive and Negative Qualities
(John M. Dusay)

(d) Complex Ego State Diagram
(Mary and Robert Goulding)

(e) An Egogram (John M. Dusay)

Figure 12 Functional Diagrams

So the Rebellious Child, as described by Berne, does indeed seem to be unadapted and yet not quite the same as 'Free'. Some practitioners, and even some Teachers, seem to have perceived the Free Child as wholly positive and have made no provision for the possibility that unrestrained freedom might ever be counterproductive! The New Ego State Model, however, recognizes (as does Berne elsewhere) that *Physis*, the growth force of nature which has its roots in the Somatic Child, needs care and control if it is to be 'properly nourished so that the individual has an urge to grow and to behave "better" – that is, in accordance with principles ... which take the happiness of others into consideration'.[22] In the full quotation Berne does, in fact, refer to the Superego, not to the Parent ego state. But the distinction does not, in my view, detract from the point at issue.

In the New Ego State Model, the Rebellious Child might be an adaptation to restraints emanating from Mother's or Father's Child ego state (P1) or else a Child which either has been allowed unfettered freedom or has successfully rejected Control by the Nurturing Parent (P2) of Mother and Father.

Figure 12(c) is John M. Dusay's functional diagram in his book *Egograms*.[54] The first difference between this and Figure 12(a), is that the divisions are horizontal rather than vertical. The reason for this is evidently to facilitate a vertical line from top to bottom that divides all the ego states into positive and negative functions. He also describes the Parent ego state as having critical, rather than controlling, features, however. This does, though, provide for the positive value of criticism that most other models fail to acknowledge.

Figure 12(d): This diagram is provided by the Gouldings in *Changing Lives Through Redecision Therapy*.[18] It is, as they say, a 'complex' diagram, combining structure with function, and it illustrates structural contributions from Mother and from Father to two different elements in the Parent ego state (P2) which they describe as Critical (rather than Controlling) and Nurturing. Their illustration of the Child ego state does not differentiate between Mother's and Father's contributions to P1 and the Adapted Child ego state.

Figure 12(e) is a diagram of an 'egogram' as described by John M. Dusay in his book *Egograms*.[54] I find this a very useful diagnostic and therapeutic tool, even though it is based on Critical and Nurturing Parent ego state functions that are both supposedly elements of P2. The principle behind egograms is the 'constancy hypothesis' – the belief that each human personality contains a finite and constant amount of psychic energy. The distribution of this energy among the various functional ego states gives the personality of each individual an emotional 'shape' or profile.

While some people have tried to construct egograms on the basis of a questionnaire designed to reveal the amount of energy invested in each ego state function, these have not been very successful. Dusay says, 'The egogram is based on intuition and is logically constructed – born of the cooperation between the "feeling" and "thinking" sides of the observer'.[54] I find it possible to sketch the egogram of a person within a few minutes of meeting him or her, and experience has shown that others, familiar with this model, will usually draw a very similar profile.

Ego states, however, are like muscles in that they become stronger with exercise and weaker with neglect. This provides for the possibility of a simple therapeutic programme. For example, an overactive Adapted Child can be partially deactivated by exercises designed to divert some of the energy into, say, the Adult ego state – or, indeed, to any of the other ego state functions. To some extent, therapeutic progress can be judged by the intuitive construction of a new egogram at various stages of therapy, and contracts can then be agreed to divert more energy into those ego state functions that are seen to be deficient.

Claude Steiner, who identifies the Critical Parent with P1, as I do, and sees the entire Parent ego state (P2) as normally nurturing in function and valuable, has constructed an egogram that attempts to take these considerations into account. He introduces the Little Professor (A1), however, as a column in the bar graph and thereby adds to the confusion because the Little Professor functions only in partnership with either the Free Child or the Adapted Child. It is partly for this reason that I have not included egograms in the main text in Chapter 2. There is, however, no reason why an egogram should not be constructed out of the elements in the New Ego State Model. This can include the Care (Cr) as well as the Control (Cl) elements of the Nurturing Parent, the Adult, the Adapted Child, and the Natural or Free Child. The Demon, or Unsocialized Natural Child, can be included in addition if the client manifests that element, as antisocial clients often do.

Appendix B
Developmental History

A Developmental History is a mini-autobiography. The client is provided with a set of A4 sheets, each sheet ruled into fifteen squares. The first square is numbered 0, which is the year of birth, in the top left-hand corner; the second is numbered 1, and so on to as many as are necessary.

Notes for the Preparation of a Developmental History

Each of the squares on the sheets represents one year of your life. Note, in the appropriate year, anything you think might be of significance for your development. These will be experiences which you think probably had some important emotional impact on you. For example:

- At your birth: were you one of twins? the first child of your parents? wanted or unwanted? planned or accidental? adopted? a sickly child? etc.

- It doesn't matter where you went for your holidays when you were six, but it could be important if you got lost on the beach and it was a long time before your parents found you.

- Other important things might be, for example:
  I was in hospital for X weeks/months/years at age X.
  My mother was in hospital for …
  I was very ill/had a serious accident …
  My brother/sister was a sick child and got all the attention.
  I was assaulted/abused …
  I fell in love and …
  My parents split …
  I set up home with …

Significant events connected with school, college, work, etc., should be noted.

Don't be too anxious about exactly what age things happened, unless you know the age is specially important. The sequence of events might be more significant. Write things across two age-spaces or more if you're uncertain about dates.

The important things in your developmental history are those that affected the way you felt about yourself and about other people, and your perception of the world. If you are not even sure what really happened, it might be important to record what you believe happened. If something might have happened which you are not ready to talk about put an asterisk (*).

You might not be able to complete the Developmental History all in one go. Add to it from time to time. Bring it with you to counselling sessions, to refer to and also to add to if anything new emerges. There is no reason why you should not discuss life events with family members if you wish.

Appendix C
A Brief Questionnaire
for Character Disorder

Each item is merely a basis for enquiry. One 'starter' question is suggested in each case. Diagnostically, the questionnaire is best used without the client's knowledge, though it might be shared later. It might also be helpful to ask the client to answer the questions himself to compare his self-assessment with the counsellor's. The counsellor's assessment will, in any event, usually be largely intuitive and this should *always* be checked out as far as possible.

Circle the number on the right that best matches your assessment. Any items assessed at 3 or 4 give ground for considering character disorder or character neurotic as possible diagnoses, even if other scores are low. Otherwise, total scores up to about 14 might indicate no significant character disorder; 15 to 26 suggests moderate, 27 to 40 is severe. This is a diagnostic tool but not a scientific instrument.

1 Impulsiveness   1   2   3   4
 (*What important decisions have you taken on the spur of the moment?*)

2 Inclination to deceive   1   2   3   4
 (*In what situations would you think it appropriate to conceal the truth?*)

3 Failure to make long-term, committed relationships   1   2   3   4
 (*How many long-term relationships have you had and for how long?*)

4 Pursuit of excitement   1   2   3   4
 (*What kind of **risky** activities do you enjoy? e.g., sport, gambling, etc.*)

5 Lack of commitment to a belief system 1   2   3   4
   (*What beliefs – such as politics, religion,*
   philosophy – influence your life style?)

6 Lack of self control   1   2   3   4
   (*Which feelings do you have most*
   difficulty controlling?)

7 Reluctance to accept authority   1   2   3   4
   (*How do you feel and behave when people*
   in charge give you orders?)

8 Addiction   1   2   3   4
   (*How much use do you make of alcohol,*
   gambling, drugs, pornography?)

9 Failure to care for others   1   2   3   4
   (*What sacrifices or gifts do you make*
   in order to care for someone else?)

10 Untrustworthiness   1   2   3   4
   (*How much do you trust yourself?*)

Appendix D
Some Questions to Ask Yourself

This book is not designed to be a 'self-help' book. Nevertheless, those wishing to become practising counsellors, either professional or voluntary, must gain insight into their own emotional processes and so must undergo personal therapy or counselling. Without this, they are in constant danger of confusing the client's needs with their own, without realizing what is happening. Addressing the questions below, and answering them thoughtfully, might help readers to understand the text and to identify some of those areas of their own lives that need to be explored in more depth, perhaps in the course of personal work.

Additionally, questions such as these can usefully be addressed to the client, perhaps in the context of teaching him basic TA.

1 Which of your ego states (*see* New Ego State Model) seems most to influence the kind of person you are? (Chapters 1 and 2.)

2 What kind of positive Strokes do you most readily give to others? (Chapter 4.)

3 What kind of positive Strokes do you feel you need? (Chapter 4.)

4 What kind of Strokes does someone close to you really need? Are you meeting those needs? If not, is the person really 'alive'? (Chapter 4.)

5 Which of the Time Structures do you use most often? (Chapter 4.)

6 How useful is your preferred Time Structure in getting you Positive Strokes? (Chapter 4.)

7 Do you tend to play psychological Games from the starting role of Persecutor, Rescuer, or Victim? (Chapter 5.)

8 Which role do you usually finish in? (Chapter 5.)

9 How readily do you experience and express *appropriate* joy, anger, fear, and sadness? (Chapter 2, New Ego State Model, and Chapter 5.)

10 What Racket Feelings do you experience most often as substitutes for appropriate and useful feelings – especially at the end of a psychological Game? (Chapters 4 and 5.)

11 Which of the three Not-OK Life Positions do you tend to take refuge in when the going gets rough? (Chapter 7.)

12 Which of the twelve Injunctions seem to have been most damaging to your personal well-being? (Chapter 8.)

13 Which of the five Drivers affect your life-style most significantly? (Chapter 8.)

14 What Early Decisions do you think you might have made as a youngster which you are still holding to now, when they are no longer useful? (Chapter 8.)

15 Which of the 'passive behaviours' do you tend to use as a means of *not* solving problems? (Chapter 9.)

16 What might you need to change about yourself if you are to achieve your full potential as a total human being? (Chapters 10, 11, and 12.)

17 What kind of suffering do you seek to avoid, rather than face up to authentically? (Chapter 14 .)

Appendix E
Further Training in Transactional Analysis

Introductory courses in Transactional Analysis are being offered quite widely by colleges and universities, and in evening classes. Often these are not conducted by qualified and experienced practitioners of TA, although the teachers may well be qualified in other styles of counselling. Anyone thinking of becoming a Transactional Analyst, however, (or, ideally, even seriously considering practising TA as part of a more eclectic service) should seek out a Teaching and Supervising Transactional Analyst (TSTA) or a practitioner who is training to become one (PTSTA) and is authorized provisionally to teach trainees up to CTA (Certified Transactional Analyst) standard.

TSTAs and PTSTAs usually offer a variety of courses, sometimes led by guest trainers from the United States, Europe, or elsewhere. In addition to Transactional Analysis, such courses might be in Gestalt Therapy, Neuro-Linguistic Programming (NLP), dreamwork, or many other styles of working, which are usually compatible with TA and used by TA practitioners as a normal feature of their work.

The first step on the road to certification as a Transactional Analyst is to attend a 101 Introductory Course led by an authorized Teacher or Instructor. This is usually a two-day event involving twelve hours of training which give an overview of all basic Transactional Analysis theory. At the end of it the participant receives a 101 Certificate which is required before he or she can proceed to the next stage in advanced training. It is also possible to obtain this Certificate by sitting a written exam without attending a 101 Introductory Course.

Armed with the 101 Certificate, the would-be trainee can then seek sponsorship for training by a TSTA or PTSTA. Before agreeing to this, the Teacher will almost certainly want to have some non-contractual experience of working with the applicant. This would involve regular supervision in which tape-recorded or video-recorded segments of actual therapeutic work are brought to the Teacher for comment and discussion. When the Teacher is satisfied that the applicant is likely to succeed in qualifying, a contract will be arranged, usually for an initial period of three years, which can be extended if necessary. During this period, the trainee must complete a very considerable number of hours of practice, training, supervision, and personal therapy. The minimum period of training, even for psychiatrists and clinical psychologists, who will be extensively trained and experienced already, is eighteen months before taking the final examination.

All this is very expensive, especially if the trainee has to travel a long way to see the Teacher and to attend workshops by other people, which often entail overnight accommodation. Some trainees will be working with public services or voluntary agencies, and treating their clients without fees. But, even if the trainee can afford to pay the several thousands of pounds that full training will cost, additional work, probably in the evenings, on a fee-paying basis is advisable if only to have clients who are sufficiently well motivated to be willing to pay.

Certification is, first, by written examination which is usually a detailed case study in which the candidate demonstrates theoretical knowledge and its practical application. When the Teacher judges that the trainee is ready – probably after one or more 'mock exams' – the Final Oral Examination, often held in another country, is conducted by a Board of four Advanced Members. It is a relatively informal, but nevertheless searching, examination lasting about an hour. After presenting and discussing a detailed record of the candidate's experience, brief tape-recorded segments of professional work are presented to the Board, whose members will then ask questions of the candidate to ascertain his or her standard of competence. A 'beginning practitioner' is not expected to be perfect in all respects! No one 'fails' but if the candidate is not found to be up to an acceptable standard, then he or she will be 'deferred' and can appear before a Board again later.

Those who pass the Board become CTAs – that is Certified Transactional Analysts. Certification may now be in four areas of specialization – Clinical, Organizational, Educational, or Counselling.

If the candidate then wishes to proceed with further training with a view to becoming a Teaching and Supervising Transactional Analyst or an Instructor (authorized to present 101 Introductory Courses but not to contract for advanced teaching), the next step is to attend a Training Endorsement Workshop. Once authorized to be a Provisional Training and Supervising Transactional Analyst (under contractual training to a TSTA), the candidate can then be 'in business' as a recognized teacher of Transactional Analysis.

Accreditation as a Certified Transactional Analyst, with a clinical or counselling speciality, provides the basic hours of training, practical application, and personal therapy required for accreditation with the British Association for Counselling. Further requirements must also be fulfilled, however, such as case studies and agreement for regular contractual supervision by a properly qualified colleague. Professional Members of the Institute of Transactional Analysis, accredited by either the International Transactional Analysis Association (ITAA) or the European Association for Transactional Analysis (EATA), are eligible for registration as Transactional Analysis Psychotherapists with the government-recognized United Kingdom Council for Psychotherapy (UKCP). Several TSTAs and PTSTAs now have arrangements with universities so that trainees, on qualifying as Certified Transactional Analysts, can also graduate with a Master's degree, perhaps after completion of an acceptable dissertation.

The Institute of Transactional Analysis publishes the *ITA News* three times a year. This contains professional articles and is also a mine of information about UK-authorized Teachers, training courses and workshops, 101 Introductory Courses, Regional Representatives, Study/Peer Groups, classified advertising, details of ITA Council members and other contacts, and many other features.

The Institute of Transactional Analysis is an organization but not a building. Trainees do not attend a specific college for a period of months or years but are contracted to a teacher who will guide them in finding a variety of training opportunities that might be in a variety of places. The ITA can, however, be contacted through its Administrator whose telephone number can be obtained through BT Directory Enquiries.

References

1. Midgley, David (Spring and Autumn, 1993) 'Character Disorder – A TA Perspective', *ITA News*.
2. Berne, Eric (1968) *Games People Play*. London: Penguin.
3. Berne, Eric (1975) *Transactional Analysis in Psychotherapy*. London: Sovereign Press.
4. Steiner, Claude (1974) *Scripts People Live*. New York: Grove Press.
5. Berne, Eric (1975) *What Do You Say After You Say Hello?* London: Corgi.
6. Goleman, Daniel (1996) *Emotional Intelligence*. London: Bloomsbury.
7. *Collins English Dictionary* (1979) London and Glasgow: Collins.
8. *Stones Justices Manual* (1992); Children and Young Persons Act, Sec. 1, Subsec. 2(d) and S.70(1); Children Act, 1969, 3(i); 2(b)(11).
9. Steiner, Claude (1971) *Games Alcoholics Play*. New York: Grove Press.
10. Weiss, Jon and Laurie (1977) 'Corrective Parenting in Private Practice' in Graham Barnes (ed.) *TA After Eric Berne*. New York: Harpers College Press.
11. Midgley, David (Spring 1996) 'Halifax', *ITA News*, No. 44.
12. Thomas, George (1983) 'Fear, Anger and Sadness', *Trans. Anal. Jnl.*, January.
13. Erskine, Richard G. and Zalcman, M. (1979) 'The Racket System, a Model for Racket Analysis', *Trans. Anal. Jnl.*, January.
14. Ware, Paul (1983) 'Personality Adaptations (Doors to Therapy)', *Trans. Anal. Jnl.*, January.
15. Stewart, Ian (1996) *Developing TA Counselling*. London: Sage Publications.
16. Woollams, Stan and Brown, Michael (1978) *Transactional Analysis*. Michigan: Huron Valley Institute Press.
17. English, Fanita (1969) 'Episcript and the "hot potato" game', *Trans. Anal. Bulletin* 8, 32.

18. Goulding, Robert and Mary (1997) *Changing Lives Through Redecision Therapy.* New York: Brunner/Mazel.
19. Kahler, Taibi and Capers, Hedges (1974) 'The Miniscript', *Trans. Anal. Jnl.*, January.
20. Kahler, Taibi (1978) *Transactional Analysis Revisited.* Little Rock, Arkansas: Human Development Pubs.
21. Stewart, Ian and Joines, Vann (1987) *TA To-Day.* Nottingham: Life Space Publishing.
22. Berne, Eric (1971) *A Layman's Guide to Psychiatry and Psychoanalysis.* London: Penguin.
23. Clarkson, Petruska (1992) '*Physis* in Transactional Analysis', *ITA News* 33, Summer.
24. Clarkson, Petruska (1992) *Transactional Analysis Psychotherapy – an Integrated Approach.* London: Routledge.
25. Schiff, Jacqui with Day, Beth (1970) *All My Children.* Philadelphia: Evans.
26. Schiff, Jacqui, et al. (1975) *Cathexis Reader, TA Treatment of Psychosis.* New York: Harper & Row.
27. Rycroft, Charles (1968) *A Critical Dictionary of Psychoanalysis.* London: Nelson.
28. Freud, Sigmund (1949) *An Outline of Psychoanalysis.* London: Hogarth Press.
29. WHO (1978) ICD 9 *Glossary and Guide to Classification of Diseases.* World Health Organization.
30. APA (1994) *Diagnostic and Statistical Manual DSM IV.* American Psychiatric Association.
31. Clarkson, Petruska (1992) 'In Praise of Speed, Experimentation, Agreeableness, Endurance and Excellence: Counterscript Drivers and Aspiration', *Trans. Anal. Jnl.*, January.
32. Dennis, Norman and Erdos, George (1992) *Families Without Fatherhood.* London: IEA Health and Welfare Unit.
33. Klein, Mavis (1991) *OK Parenting, A Psychological Handbook.* London: Piatkus Publishing.
34. Peck, M. Scott (1990) *The Road Less Travelled.* London: Arrow.
35. Brown, Michael (1977) *Psychodiagnosis in Brief.* Ypsilanti, MI: Spectrum Psychological Service.
36. Perls, Frederick S. (1969) *Gestalt Therapy Verbatim.* Moab, Utah: Real People Press.
37. Hoghughi, Masud (1980) *Assessing Problem Children.* London: Sage.
38. Hoghughi, Masud (1988) *Treating Problem Children.* London: Andre Deutsch.
39. Schiff, Shea, Workshop Presentation, 1983.

40. Midgley, David (1992) *Taking Charge of Your Own Life.* Middlesbrough: New Directions Publishing.
41. Wheelis, Allen (1975) *How People Change.* New York: Harper Colophon.
42. James, Muriel (1976) *Techniques in Transactional Analysis.* Reading, MA: Addison-Wesley.
43. Robinson, Isobel, J. Personal Communication.
44. Glauberman, Dina (1989) *Life Choices and Life Changes Through Image Work.* London: Unwin.
45. Stewart, Ian (1989) *Transactional Analysis Counselling in Action.* London: Sage.
46. James, Muriel (1985) *It's Never Too Late to be Happy — The Psychology of Self-Reparenting.* Reading, MA: Addison-Wesley.
47. Swede, Southey (1997) *How to Cure — How Eric Berne Practiced Transactional Analysis.* San Francisco: Boyce Productions Trans. Pubs.
48. Jung, C. G. (1984) *Modern Man in Search of a Soul.* London: Ark.
49. Sheldrake, Rupert (1987) *A New Science of Life.* London: Paladin.
50. Lovelock, James (1989) *The Ages of Gaia.* Oxford: Oxford University Press.
51. Drummond, Henry (1897) *Natural Law in the Spiritual World.* London: Hodder & Stoughton.
52. Beisser, Arnold (1971) in *Gestalt Therapy Now,* Fagan and Shepherd (eds). New York: Harper Colophon.
53. James, Muriel and Jongeward, Dorothy (1971) *Born to Win.* Reading, MA: Addison-Wesley.
54. Dusay, John (1977) *Egograms.* New York: Harper & Row.

Index

Index compiled by
Sue Carlton